Arrow's Theorem: The Paradox of Social Choice

Alfred F. MacKay

ARROW'S THEOREM

THE PARADOX OF SOCIAL CHOICE

A CASE STUDY IN THE PHILOSOPHY OF ECONOMICS

Yale University Press, New Haven and London, 1980

Designed by James J. Johnson
and set in VIP Optima type.
Printed in the United States of America by
Halliday Lithograph, West Hanover, Mass.

Library of Congress Cataloging in Publication Data

MacKay, Alfred F.
  Arrow's theorem, the paradox of social choice.

  Includes index.
  1. Welfare economics.   I. Title.
HB99.3.M23   330.15′5   79–26445
ISBN 0–300–02450–9
ISBN 0–300–03259–5 (pbk.)

10   9   8   7   6   5   4   3   2

Contents

Preface

This book is subtitled, "A Case Study in the Philosophy of Economics." A word of explanation is in order. Since as far as I know there is no such field as the philosophy of economics, at least no past familiarity with it should create false expectations. Still, bearing in mind the distinction occasionally drawn (for example) between philosophy of language and philosophy of linguistics —where whatever the former is, the latter studies the methodology and conceptual foundations of empirical linguistics—one might suppose that the present work would occupy the latter side of the "philosophy of" divide. It won't. Much as a discussion of space and time might be called philosophy of science rather than philosophy of physics—to neutralize a similar suggestion of narrow, foundational critique—so the present work might be termed philosophy of social science rather than philosophy of economics. But that would mislead in the other direction. Philosophy of social science, as reflected in introductory textbooks and collections of readings, is like Henry Ford in offering the customer his choice of topic as long as it is methodology. The present work utters, I hope, not a methodological word.

This book is a case study of a problem involved in attempting to combine individual preferences into collective choice. Its subject matter thus overlaps several disciplines—political theory, welfare economics, decision theory, ethics, political philosophy, philosophy of action, and even theoretical psychology and sociology—as regards their concern with measurement and manipulation of psychological phenomena. Notwithstanding this multidisciplinary image, the original demonstration of the major result in this area (Arrow's Theorem) was done by an economist in the context of welfare economics. And, without meaning to belittle the important contributions of others, most subsequent developments have been due to economists. Hence, this book is called a case study in the philosophy of economics. It is not a philosophical critique of the science of economics: its foundations, methodology, and prospects for salvation. It is a philosophical treatment of a problem, or set of issues, that has been located mainly, if not exclusively, in economics. It contains what some would call *applied philosophy*.

Fairness dictates acknowledging that I am interested in Arrow's impossibility result (as the problem has come to be known) for its own sake, and not exclusively as a thing to avoid. I seek to explain why it works, what makes it tick, and to do so in a way that removes the air of paradox. Thus, to anticipate a bit, even if it could be shown that one or more of Arrow's conflict-generating requirements was not really a clear demand of rationality, it would still be of interest to understand why we could not have them all if we happened to want them. I mention this early because it is a view not universally shared. Some people, especially economists and political theorists, appear to be interested in Arrow's theorem only insofar as they see it as a threat or impediment to something else which they are really interested in. Thus, they want to think about it only as long as it takes to find a way around it. I, by contrast, adopt what I take to have been Lord Russell's position: that a good paradox is a thing to be treasured; that from reflecting on and attempting to unravel it much can be learned which might be missed from too great a hurry to get on with "more important things." Whether that was Lord Russell's view or not, it is the one taken here.

Our approach will be as nonmathematical as the subject permits. It will perforce involve proofs and reflections on proofs, but no manipulations of numbers, or reasonings employing the calculus. And in the treatment of proofs, and generally through-out, every attempt has been made to substitute words and sen-tences for symbols and formulas, and hence to conduct the rea-soning in civilized rather than symbolized English. Thus, it is intended that the qualifications required of the reader be applied intelligence, not applied mathematics. I do not mean by this to be taking a position on the vexed question of the place of mathe-matics in the social sciences, nor is this a matter of condescend-ing to the lazy or the literary. Mathematical analyses provide their own special illumination, but they do not provide the only sort. In my view there are now enough wholly admirable mathe-matical treatises on social choice to satisfy any reasonable de-mand. Of the making of proofs and variations on proofs, of the getting of slightly different results from marginal adjustments to axioms, there is no end and it becomes a great weariness. But of treatments accessible to the interested nonspecialist, of explana-tions in addition to demonstrations, and of discursive reasoning to supplement the mathematical, there remains a need.

Portions of this work appear elsewhere. I thank the editors of *The Journal of Philosophy* for permission to use material from my "Interpersonal Comparisons," vol. 72 (1975); the editors of *Theory and Decision* for permission to use material from "Prefer-ence Anarchy," vol. 11 (1979) by E. Wong and myself; and the International Amateur Athletic Federation for permission to re-produce a page from their *Scoring Table for Men's Track and Field Events* (Portmadoc, Caernarvonshire: The Snowdonia Press, 1971).

I am grateful to Oberlin College for granting me Research Sta-tus and to the American Council of Learned Societies for a fel-lowship that allowed me the time and support to think through and write down an early draft. To my friends, colleagues, and students for stimulation and to my wife and family for encourage-ment I am considerably indebted.

1

Social Choice and Arrow's Paradox

The *problem of social choice* is this: How can many individuals' preferences be combined to yield a collective choice? Various procedures have been, or might be, proposed to accomplish this feat, all of which differ from each other in many respects. We will call such procedures (mechanisms, combination rules) *aggregation devices*, or sometimes just *devices*. In democratic political theory, for example, the various possible voting schemes are all simply aggregation devices. The *theory of social choice* studies aggregation devices: what they are; how they work; how they differ; what they presuppose and imply; what can be said for and against the principal types; whether there is a perfect or ideal type, and if so, what features it has; and so on. Thus far, the main results of this theory have been discouragingly negative. In the early 1950s the distinguished economist (now Nobel Laureate) Kenneth J. Arrow showed, in a demonstration that has come to be called Arrow's Impossibility Theorem, that given certain plausible assumptions, there can be no ideally rational aggregation device. We will, in this book, attempt to come to terms with Arrow's justly famous result. We will try to explain what it is, understand why and how it works, examine its implications, and consider suggestions for evading it.

The present work contains little that is new concerning the technicalities of this area. It attempts no major contribution to the

1

mathematics of the problem. Our approach is that Arrow's Theorem presents a fascinating problem in the philosophy of economics. It wears on its face that paradoxical aspect which is the hallmark of so many philosophical problems. It arises from a priori, conceptual sources, and provides scope for investigation by reflection and analysis rather than exclusively by experimentation. It has a good claim to be considered the outstanding problem in the philosophy of economics.

What, then, is Arrow's Theorem? Without now going into the details, Arrow proves, as we said, that it is impossible to construct a "rational" aggregation device. But there are many extant aggregation devices: for example, the voting systems in use every day. So everything depends on what is meant by "rational." The content of that notion is partially specified by four very general conditions which Arrow claims it is reasonable to require any aggregation device to meet. These seem almost innocuous, they are so weak. (Weakness is a virtue here. The weaker such constraints are, the less you have to take on faith when accepting them.) Listing them by name only, for future reference, they are:

(U) Unrestricted scope.
(P) Pareto principle.
(D) Nondictatorship.
(I) Independence of irrelevant alternatives.[1]

1. I follow Arrow's more economical presentation in "Values and Collective Decision-Making," in P. Laslett and W. G. Runciman, eds., *Philosophy, Politics, and Society*, 3d ser. (New York: Barnes & Noble, 1967), and in the 2d edition of *Social Choice and Individual Values* (New Haven, Conn.: Yale University Press, 1963), chap. 8, sec. 2. In his original monograph, *Social Choice and Individual Values* (New Haven, Conn.: Yale University Press, 1951), there were five conditions. The terminology (U), (P), (D), and (I) is from A. K. Sen, *Collective Choice and Social Welfare* (San Francisco: Holden-Day, 1970), sec. 3.3. Sometimes I call Condition (U) "Unlimited scope."

Arrow shows that no device can jointly satisfy four apparently reasonable requirements, and in that sense no reasonable or "rational" aggregation device is possible. Since his proof is nondefective (that is, formally valid), this naturally concentrates attention upon those four requirements. Indeed, one's evaluation of the "importance" of Arrow's result will depend in large measure upon one's assessment of the plausibility of his four conditions. If, as he sometimes suggests, they do embody canons of rationality—if, to use older language, they are clear dictates of reason—then his impossibility result takes on one aspect. If, on the other hand, one or more of them has some hidden flaw or can be forgone at small or no cost, then it takes on a different aspect.

Before turning to a detailed plausibility assessment, a process that will engage us throughout this work, it might be useful to locate Arrow's enterprise on the conceptual map, and to make various comparisons and contrasts, chiefly in the history of recent ethics. It has been said that anyone familiar with this somewhat depressing history will know that whenever you have even two independent, basic principles, they conflict. So why should it be surprising that Arrow shows how four taken together do? Arguments to the effect that certain very fundamental evaluative claims—each of which seems when independently considered to commend itself to right reason—in fact conflict and are logically incompatible, are staple fare in the history of ethics.[2] Why, then, should Arrow's very similar project cause such a stir?

Part of the answer may be that his work was not directed toward an audience of historians of philosophy, but toward economists and decision theorists. Such an audience is understandably

2. See, for example, Henry Sidgwick's Methods of Ethics, 7th ed. (London: MacMillan and Company, 1907), and W. D. Ross's The Right and the Good (Oxford: Oxford University Press, 1930).

ignorant of the disappointments, the "impossibility theorems," the generally negative results of classical modern ethics. So, like all reinventions of the wheel, Arrow's result astonishes the innocent. This, whether true or not, is not a sufficient explanation.

Another part of the answer might involve the ingenuity, the genius, displayed in devising a mathematically tractable formulation of a difficult and complex issue, rendering it susceptible of rigorous proof as opposed to persuasive argument. Again, no one familiar with standards of argument in moral philosophy, which, whether due to the intrinsic nature of the subject (only admitting of so much exactitude, as Aristotle claimed), or to the limitations of its practitioners, or to some other cause, contains a proportion of persuasion to proof that is perhaps higher than in any other area of philosophy, can fail to be impressed by the magnitude of this aspect of Arrow's achievement. It is an accomplishment not even approached in philosophical ethics, where the debate between utilitarians and intuitionists still continues, concerning in part whether there really is a conflict between the principle of utility and the precepts of justice. There can be no similar lingering doubts about the existence of a conflict among Arrow's four requirements. Settling that part of the question once and for all is a great leap forward. A similar advance in ethics would constitute that will-o'-the-wisp, Progress in Philosophy. Arrow's treatment of the conceptual problems of social choice stands, in this respect, as a model of the way some philosophical issues can be posed and occasionally brought to definitive resolution.

A related point is that Arrow's formal, axiomatic approach has the usual benefits regarding direction of further inquiry. In the first place, it forces exposure of operative assumptions and makes them relatively accessible to close examination. If the proof is valid—and it is—then the natural place to turn for further inquiry is to the premises. And there they all are, in plain view, clearly and exactly expressed. Furthermore, as we shall see, by exposing the formal structure of the argument, the axiomatic formulation aids in distinguishing form from content. This, in turn, enables reinterpretation of the normal content in nonstandard ways, often with illuminating results.

But important as these considerations are, they still do not adequately capture the boldness of Arrow's result. Its most striking feature is how unexpected and unobvious it is. To use an example from the history of ethics, everyone knew there was at least a prima facie conflict between duty and utility (or, expedience, as it is often termed), so it came as no great surprise when Sidgwick, and later Ross, argued its existence so forcefully. The naked, aggressive thrust for maximum utility plainly threatens the niceties of our stations and their duties. There, the challenging task is to construct a secular, ethical theodicy which harmonizes the apparent conflict—thus the attractions of rule-utilitarianism. With Arrow's Theorem, on the other hand, not only was the disclosed four-element conflict not widely suspected in advance, but even after thoroughly digesting the proof it can hardly be believed. His result is, in this broad sense, paradoxical. Although his four conditions demonstrably do conflict, one cannot (except for rehearsing the proof itself) see *why* they should. This, perhaps, finally accounts for the impact of Arrow's Theorem. It is a rigorous demonstration of an entirely unobvious, surprising, paradoxical result. Like all the great paradoxes, Arrow's result on collective rationality resists understanding and resolution equally as it demands the attempt.[3]

With these preliminaries behind us, let us turn to one of the problems discussed by Arrow. When we say that aggregation devices are rules or procedures for generating social choice based

3. Omitted here, obviously, are more mundane considerations of "importance": that Arrow's Theorem allegedly sounds the death knell of democratic theory, welfare economics, and various other good things. As J. L. Austin once remarked, "Importance isn't important. Truth is." We have only attempted to account for the *intellectual* fascination of Arrow's result, not all the variously motivated attention it has drawn.

on individual preferences, we have not said very much. The notion of one thing's being "based on" something else is so open-ended that it cries out for further specification. One ultimate, overall aim of studies of social choice is to characterize good, desirable, or even acceptable aggregation devices. To do that, we have to say more than merely that the social output must be "based on" individual inputs. But what?

To see the problem, consider what Arrow dubs an "illfare" function, an aggregation procedure that completely reverses the individuals' preferences—that is, when everybody prefers X to Y, the device generates the social choice Y over X. Such a system would feature one, albeit perverse, way of basing social choice on individual preferences. So even if we are not prepared to legislate in advance the details of what any acceptable device will have to be like, we will surely want to say something about what, broadly speaking, we might call its directionality. Or again, consider a device that automatically reproduces the preferences of some one person and designates them as the social choice. This would feature another perverse way of "basing" social choice on individual preference. And again, while not prescribing matters of detail, we might wish to require that the social choice be, in some sense, a genuinely collective affair.

It is at this very high level of generality that Arrow's four constraints operate. They represent normative judgments—requirements that embody a conception of the way aggregation devices ought and ought not to be. Yet they are, unlike many value judgments we can imagine in this area (for example, that a voting system ought to demand at least a three-fifths majority) relatively uncontroversial. Of course, they purchase their wide acceptability at the price of apparently innocuous minimality. They seem to be extremely weak requirements, leaving many important questions perfectly open, closing off only what may seem ridiculously perverse options. No doubt a full characterization of desirability or acceptability for aggregation devices would need to include many more, and more specific, detailed constraints than these beginning four. But, as Arrow remarks, these are more than enough. He proves that no aggregation device can jointly satisfy even these:

1. (U) The first requirement is (U), *unrestricted scope*. This requires that an acceptable device be able to process any (logically) coherent set of individual preference rankings of any number of choice alternatives.[4]

Finitism is not particularly at issue here. All that Arrow's proof requires is at least three voters who can order three alternatives any way they please. On the face of it this requirement seems plausible enough. If you are going to consult the wishes of the multitude at all, you may as well let them express whatever preferences they really have, for whatever alternatives they happen to be faced with, under no artificially imposed restraints. One can imagine, of course, devices which only permit social choice between certain special, or special-sized, groups of alternatives, or which only accept certain preferred preference patterns as in-

---

4. In *Social Choice and Individual Values*, Arrow calls his first requirement *collective rationality*. It includes, in addition to (U), a stipulation that preference and indifference be logically well behaved, that is, that they at least be transitive and connected. [What this means is that if alternative X is preferred (indifferent) to alternative Y, and Y in turn is preferred (indifferent) to Z, then X must be preferred (indifferent) to Z. That is what transitivity is. Connectedness means that for any two alternatives X and Y, either X is preferred to Y, or Y to X, or they are indifferent.] In the present work, logical well behavedness will be treated as a standing background assumption in order to concentrate attention on those aspects of Arrow's requirements that can intuitively be thought of as constraining the device itself. It is, however, true and worth keeping in mind that Arrow's result can be evaded by tinkering in various ways with the logical features of the preference relations; or, as some would say, by changing the subject.

put. But it seems prima facie unreasonable to put up with such limitations if we can stipulate unrestricted scope, thus getting the preferred patterns and all the rest too.

2. (P) The second requirement is (P), the *Pareto principle*. This requires that when every individual without exception prefers X to Y, the device must rank X above Y in its social ordering. That is, whatever else it may do, an acceptable device must honor unanimity.

It is difficult to see how the social choice could be said to reflect individual preferences or be responsive to them in any significant sense if it failed to ratify unanimous consensus. Argument can arise over differences, but unanimity seems unquestionable. This requirement amounts to an exceedingly weak constraint on what we earlier called the *directionality* of the "based on" relation. Its innocuous weakness, and hence its relative uncontroversiality, springs from this: the only additional specification it applies to the vague notion of social choice's being based on individual preferences is that however "based on" gets embodied in detail, a device must implement unanimity.

3. (D) The third requirement is (D), *nondictatorship*. This prohibits an acceptable device from taking the preferences of any single individual and automatically making them the social ordering regardless of the preferences of all other individuals.

This enforces the judgment that an acceptable aggregation device should be a *collective* choice procedure, not merely rubber stamping one-person rule. Although clearly an evaluative postulate, the values it embodies seem uncontroversial.

4. (I) The final requirement is (I), the *independence of irrelevant alternatives*. This requires that the social ordering of a given set of alternatives depend only on the individuals' preference orderings of those alternatives.

The effect of this requirement is to place certain constraints on the information that an acceptable device can respond to. The social output of an aggregation device, we said, is to be "based on" individual preferences. But what aspects of individuals' preferences shall it respond to in thus "basing" its social ordering? Requirement (I) provides a twofold answer to this question. First, the social ordering of an acceptable device shall depend on, and only on, preference *orderings*. By this is meant that the device shall respond only to information concerning what is preferred, and what indifferent, to what. It shall not, for example, respond to how much one thing is preferred to another (that is, not to preference intensity information), nor to any other type of information. The first part of (I), then, requires that only the bare ordering of individuals' preferences is to be taken into account. The second part says that even among individuals' preference orderings, only a restricted class of them is to be responded to. In generating a social ranking of a given set of alternatives, only preference orderings of *those alternatives* (and no others) are to be taken into account.

In summary, (I) incorporates two prohibitions: (1) the social ranking of a set of alternatives shall not depend on anything other than preference orderings, and (2) it shall not depend on preference orderings for alternatives not in that set—so-called "irrelevant" alternatives. To these two negative prohibitions it adds the positive injunction that the social ordering of a set of alternatives *shall* depend on the individuals' preference orderings of alternatives in that set.

So much for what (I) requires. Why it should be thought a plausible requirement, let alone a dictate of reason, is another matter, to which we will return in due course. The first part of it, the ordinality injunction, has in its favor whatever is to be said for ordinality versus cardinality in the treatment of preference matters generally. This includes a mixed collection of considerations involving behaviorism, observability, and the proper scientific treatment of social phenomena, which we shall not pursue at this point. Theory aside, though, this much can be said on practical grounds alone: searching for reliable, direct, preference-intensity indicators seems to be chasing what cannot be caught. There is a certain plausibility in restricting oneself to what is possible. The plausibility of the second part of (I) will be examined extensively later. From one point of view its function is subservient to that of its mate. When joined to the first (ordinality) aspect, it serves to prevent any, even indirect, recourse to cardinality. The way this works is as follows. Some people have thought that even if preference-intensity information is not directly ascertainable —by introspection, say—there is nonetheless some hope of getting it in by the back door: that is, inferring it from (ordinal) information that is reliably available.

Such ways of imputing cardinality on the basis of ordinality often depend on noting how ordinally ranked alternatives are situated vis-à-vis some selected "irrelevant" alternative(s). For example, some would hold that we can infer that A prefers X to Y more intensely than does B, if A orders five alternatives, X, α, β, γ, and Y, whereas B orders those same five alternatives, α, β, γ, X, and Y. The thought is that for A, the three alternatives α, β, and γ intervene between X and Y, one of which he ranks first and the other last. Although B also prefers X to Y, he ranks them next to last and last, respectively, and places the other three alternatives ahead of them both. X and Y are immediately adjacent to each other in B's ordering, not widely separated (by three intervening ranks) as in A's. Hence, we infer that (relatively speaking) B barely prefers X to Y while A prefers X to Y more strongly. The second part of (I) frustrates this attempt to squeeze cardinal blood out of an ordinal turnip by forbidding the social ordering of any pair of alternatives to depend on information regarding any third. In socially ranking X and Y, a device can take account only of how individuals order X and Y themselves. It cannot consider how anybody ranks α, β, or γ, either vis-à-vis X or Y or anything else.

Arrow proves that it is impossible for an aggregation device with unrestricted scope, (U), to satisfy both the Pareto principle, (P), and independence of irrelevant alternatives, (I), and also be nondictatorial, (D). In other words, no device—no matter what its detailed, inner machinery—can have acceptable scope, (U), be minimally responsive to individual preferences, (P), be sensitive only to the actual ordinal rankings to which it is applied, (I), and not be dictatorial, (D). But why not? There appear to be no connections between the four conditions through which a conflict might arise. And in a sense this is so. What we are here faced with is an inconsistent quartet of requirements, no trio and no pair of which are themselves incompatible. Now it might be thought that such a four-element inconsistent set, no subset of which is itself inconsistent, simply overloads our logical attention span. That would explain why we cannot intuitively see the incompatibility that Arrow's proof establishes. However, although there must be some limits to our logical storage and processing capacity, they are not likely to occur so early in the number line. Generations of undergraduates have seen the point of the problem of evil—God is all good, all knowing, and all powerful, yet evil exists—an inconsistent quartet, no trio and no pair of which are inconsistent.

Be that as it may, a major factor contributing to the unobviousness of Arrow's result is surely this: the *content* of the four requirements is so diverse, they seem so mutually unrelated in substance, as not to provide opportunity for interaction of any kind. What can having acceptable scope have to do with not being dictatorial? What can implementing unanimous preferences have to do with responding only to preference orderings? No intuitive connections appear. The satisfaction of (U) is compatible with either (P) or non-(P), (I) or non-(I), (D) or non-(D). And similarly for the others. No one of them bears any logical relation to another, neither entailing it nor contradicting it. Yet taken together, they are incompatible.

Social Choice and Arrow's Paradox

One of the tasks that a philosophical treatment of Arrow's paradox should set itself is the resolution of its paradoxicality. We want to find a way of understanding the original four conditions, a way of thinking about them, which will help us see why they conflict. The proof shows *that* they do, but it does not contain, written on its face, the (or even, a) reason *why*. In light of seeing why the original four clash, perhaps we can better see how to avoid the impossibility result. But more on that later. Having set out what the four Arrow requirements are, and indicated briefly where their fascination lies, it is time to begin assessing their plausibility, one by one.

2

Four Conditions on Rational
Social Choice

I. A Model for Social Choice

A *social-choice situation* consists of some choosers, some choice
alternatives, some information about the choosers' preferences
for the choice alternatives, and an aggregation device that combines this individual preference information into a collective
choice. For example, in a political setting the choosers would be
voters, the choice alternatives would be candidates (or, perhaps,
issues in a referendum), the ballot sheets would provide the individual preference information, and the tabulation process would
be the aggregation device, the procedure whereby society's
ranking of the candidates was generated based on the individuals' preferences. The latter element, the aggregation device, will
differ according to the type, amount, and format of information
on the ballot sheets, and according to what it (the device) is designed to do with that information. Some devices operate on a
plurality, some on a simple majority basis; others require a per-
centage of the total vote. Some respond just to the voters' first
choice; others accept a complete preference schedule from each
voter, ranking all the candidates. Some devices use only information about preference orderings, others respond to preference-
intensity data, and so forth. The theory of social choice studies

aggregation devices (sometimes called *social-welfare functions*) with a view to deciding whether there is a perfect, or rational, or acceptable design, and what constraints such a thing should meet.

Multi-event athletic competitions (the decathlon, for instance) generally consist of some events, some competitors, some information about how the competitors perform in the various events, and an aggregation device (sometimes called a *scoring system*) which combines this information from the individual events and generates therefrom a collective, overall ranking of the competitors. The general theory of *polyathlon scoring*, if there were one, would study scoring systems with a view to deciding whether there is a perfect, or best, or rational, or acceptable design for one, and what constraints such a thing should satisfy. The two theories—social choice and polyathlon scoring—are structurally identical, so attention to the latter might prove helpful in thinking about the former. Put otherwise, the two areas—social choice, on the one hand; polyathlon scoring, on the other—provide different content (different interpretations, different models) for the same formal structure. How fruitful this observation is remains to be seen. The proof, as always, comes in the applications, but the following elaboration on the analogy should provide a prima facie case for pursuing it further.

We can think of the events in, say, a decathlon, as ten voters in a small social-choice situation. The competitors are the candidates they have to choose among. Their (the events') "preferences" are determined by the way the competitors perform in them. Less colorfully, information about the way the competitors perform in a given event plays the same role in decathlon scoring as does information about the way a given voter prefers or ranks the candidates in "scoring" an election. A scoring system takes the performance results from each of the ten events and combines them into an overall ranking of the competitors, just as an aggregation device in an election takes what we might call the "preference results" from each voter and combines them into an overall societal ranking of the candidates. But now the plot thickens. Not only do we have the indicated correspondences between these salient elements in the social-choice and polyathlon scoring settings; in addition, the fundamental relationships and claims based thereon each have their counterparts. The "victory" relations *defeats* and *ties* exactly correspond to the preference relations *prefers* and *is indifferent*. That is, first, they—or, to bypass for now certain controversial matters, their idealizations—have the same gross logical features: such things as how many items the relation in question holds between; and such defining logical features as transitivity, symmetry, reflexivity, and so forth. Second, statements that embody claims about these fundamental relations (and which in each case constitute the bulk of the information that gets aggregated) play identical roles in their respective areas. Thus, to the athletic statement:

Competitor X defeats competitor Y in the javelin throw.

corresponds the electoral statement:

Candidate X is preferred to candidate Y by voter J.T.

and to the electoral statement:

Voter H.J. is indifferent between candidates W and Z.

corresponds the athletic statement:

In the high jump, competitors W and Z tie.

Finally, just as *order of finish* in an event corresponds to *order of preference* in a voter, so *margin of victory* of one competitor over another (in some event) corresponds to *intensity* or *strength of preference* (of some voter) for one candidate over another. That is, information concerning *how badly* (or *by how much*) one competitor defeats another in a given event corresponds to information concerning *how strongly* (or *by how much*) a given voter prefers one candidate to another. Whether such information is available in both athletic and electoral settings; in what form (qualitative, quantitative, or both) it is available; and how reliably obtainable it is, are other questions to be sure. The point is that such information *if available* and used in either area would play the same role in the process of aggregating individual inputs into a collective output.

In tabular format, some of these correspondences are:

Social Choice	*Polyathlon Scoring*
Individuals	Events
Choice alternatives	Competitors
Preferences of an individual for alternatives	Performances in an event by competitors
Aggregation device	Scoring system
X is preferred to Y by E	X defeats Y in E
E is indifferent between X and Y	X and Y tie in E
E strongly prefers X to Y	X beats Y badly in E
E prefers X to Y more strongly than he prefers Z to W	In E, X beats Y worse than Z beats W
The amount by which E prefers X to Y exceeds the amount by which he prefers Z to W in the ratio 8:5	In E, the amount by which X beats Y exceeds that by which Z beats W in the ratio 8:5
Jones prefers X to Y by exactly 27 natural preference units (NPUs)	In the high jump, X beats Y by exactly 27 centimeters
Jones likes (values, assesses the subjective worth of) X precisely 46 NPUs worth	X's time in the 400-meter dash was precisely 46 seconds

As can be seen from the table, we have athletic analogues not only for preference and indifference but for ordinality and various strengths or degrees of cardinality as well.

16

So we have (conceptual) room in the athletic model to pose and discuss many of the interesting questions that can be asked about social choice. For instance, the traditional dispute between ordinalists and cardinalists becomes the issue of whether a scoring system should respond only to information about order of finish, or, additionally, to information concerning margin of victory (or intensity of defeat, so to speak). Or again, the problem of interpersonal utility comparisons becomes something like this. Even if we could get margin-of-victory information event by event, how would we use it? Victory margins are standardly measured by seconds in running events, and by centimeters and meters in jumping and throwing events. How does one compare getting beat by 0.2 second in the 100-meter dash with winning by 15 centimeters in the pole vault, or by 7.5 meters in the javelin throw?

Why are we better off to consider these questions from this novel perspective? For one thing, it is a relatively antiseptic setting which does not engage our emotions greatly. Unlike politics or economics, nobody cares much about how decathlons are scored. In other words, it does not have "relevance." Another point is just the sheer novelty of it. It engages our intuitions at different places, and our imaginations have a hard time falling into ruts. However, again, showing *that* it is fruitful is more to the point than speculating about why it is, so consider this. Taking matters at a fairly general and abstract level, it is possible to prove an athletic version of Arrow's impossibility result, namely, that there is no "rational" way to score a polyathlon. The question becomes: Is it possible to construct a scoring system for a polyathlon that will satisfy the following four requirements?

(U′) Any number of events and competitors is allowed, and the competitors can finish in any order in any event.[1]

1. As before, we suppress the logical well-behavedness assumption, this time concerning the *defeats* and *ties* relations. These, tran-

Four Conditions on Rational Social Choice

(P') If one competitor defeats another in every event, he defeats him in the overall ranking.

(D') There is no event in which the order of competitors' finish automatically becomes the overall ranking regardless of how they fare in all other events.

(I') The overall ranking of any group of competitors depends only on the order of finish of those competitors.

The demonstrable answer is: No such scoring system is possible. And while we will not present the full proof here, perhaps a scaled-down version will give the reader an idea of how such things go. Instead of (D') above, we will use a restricted variant,

(D'') There is no (despotic) event in which a competitor's defeating another—while being defeated by him in all other events—guarantees that he defeats him in the overall ranking.

And instead of all four, we will only show that (U'), (P'), and (D'') cannot be jointly satisfied.

Consider the following polyathlon [available courtesy of (U')]. There are three events, E_1, E_2, and E_3, and four competitors, p, q, w, and z, who finish in the following orders:

$$
\begin{array}{ccccc}
E_1: & p & q & w & z \\
E_2: & w & z & p & q \\
E_3: & z & p & q & w
\end{array}
$$

(In this matrix presentation, events head rows across which are displayed the order of finish of the competitors, where *occurring*

---

sitivity and connectedness, amount to this. If X beats Y and Y beats Z, then X beats Z, and similarly for tying. And for every pair of competitors, either one beats the other or they tie. As before, we note that the impossibility result can be evaded by tinkering in various ways with the logical features of these relations.

to the right of represents *being defeated by*.) Now, by (D''), a scoring system cannot allow p to defeat z in its overall ranking, on pain of making event E_1 a despot, because z beats p in all events except E_1. Nor, for similar reasons, can it allow z to defeat w, lest E_3 be a despot. Nor again, can it allow w to defeat q, lest E_2 be despotic. Now, by connectedness, if α does not defeat β, then either β defeats α or they tie. In that case, let us say that the one competitor is *at least matched by* the other. From the transitivity and connectedness of *defeats* and *ties*, it follows that the relation *being at least matched by* is itself transitive. So, as we saw, (D'') gives us that p is at least matched by z, z by w, and w by q. Hence, by transitivity, p is at least matched by q; which implies either that q defeats p or they tie. Yet p defeats q in all three events, so (P') requires that the scoring system make p defeat q in the overall ranking. Therefore, a scoring system that satisfies (U'), (P'), and (D'') must both make p defeat q and also not do so, which is impossible. Q.E.D.

The full Arrow-like result would show this: If any scoring system has unrestricted scope, implements unanimous victories, and does not permit the results from any single event to dictate its overall ranking, then its overall ranking cannot depend only on the order of finish of the competitors concerned. Why this should be so may seem equally as puzzling for polyathlon scoring as for social choice, but the interplay between the two throws interesting light now on one, now on the other.

Perhaps the most obvious difference between the social-choice (really, psychological) model and the polyathlon scoring model concerns the direction of agency. In the psychological model the individual voter is conceived of as agent. He does (or brings about, or is responsible for) the ranking of the choice alternatives. The latter are generally viewed as passive receptacles of his manipulations (not they themselves, of course, but their mental, or intentional, representatives). The individual voter *arranges* them in order of *his* preferences. They, the choice alternatives, may or may not even be animate—issues in a referendum usually are not, candidates in an election usually are—much less active in the ranking process.

The opposite is true of the athletic model. There, the competitors (which correspond to the choice alternatives) are thought of as agents who achieve through their own efforts their places (rankings) in the events. The event (which corresponds to the individual voter) is a passive receptacle upon which the accomplishments of the participants are registered.

But striking as this difference is, it is fairly superficial: a difference that does not make much difference. Cynical politicians notoriously view social choice with the natural direction of agency reversed. For them, the electorate is so many (propoganda) receptacles to be manipulated by the efforts of the candidates. Voters are thought of as essentially passive in the whole process, registering at the ballot box the achievements of the candidates in affecting them. Some candidates are better at appealing to certain classes of voters—one to the black vote, another to the hard hat/surburbia axis—just as some athletes are better at running events, some at jumping.

By contrast, the fact that there is no obvious athletic analogue for the whole apparatus of utility theory—no counterparts to the network of interconnections among preference, choice, and (imputed) attempts to maximize something[2]—may turn out to be a difference that makes a difference. Clearly, the polyathlon model is one that will bear watching. Still, we shall use if for whatever it turns out to be worth.

---

2. It is not that we cannot get numerical measures of margin of victory, the analogue of preference intensity. We can, and furthermore the numbers we get are more objective, more reliably obtainable than anything the psychological model has to offer. But they do not fit into the sort of comprehensive, explanatory framework that cardinal utility indices, if available, would.

II. Assessing Arrow's Four Conditions

Our project then is to employ this model in assessing the independent plausibility of Arrow's four conflict-generating requirements. By "independent plausibility" is meant reason for and against each one considered separately, on its own merits, exclusive of its being implicated in the Arrow paradox. This latter factor, after all, touches each equally and hence provides no ground for choosing between them. We shall be particularly concerned with the question of whether, and to what extent, these requirements embody canons of rationality. We begin by considering their polyathlon analogues, in the order in which they appear least controversial.

> Requirement (D'), nondictatorship: The scoring system does not automatically make the results from any one event its overall ranking, regardless of how the competitors fare in all other events.

In other words, there is no event such that an athlete's performance in it determines his overall standing no matter what happens in other events. A simple, straightforward rationale for (D') is easily forthcoming. What would be the point of running all those other events if the results from one were all that mattered? Why not just run the favored (dictatorial) event and be done with it? There is nothing intrinsically wrong with holding a competition in one event only. There is nothing irrational, for instance, in running and scoring a lone 100-meter dash. But the point of doing so is presumably different from the point of holding and scoring a polyathlon. To hold and score a decathlon, say, when the outcome of the whole thing is automatically determined by the results of the 100-meter dash, the other events not affecting the outcome at all, is to render all that other activity—the running, judging, reporting of the other nine events—peculiarly pointless.

21

Four Conditions on Rational Social Choice

By "the point" of holding a polyathlon is meant what might be called its "formal or essential point," that which is implicated in the concept itself. This is to be distinguished from some person or group's de facto aim. This latter might be, for example, to distract the athletes' attention so that their spouses can escape, or to amuse the emperor's cousin, or some such extraneous thing. It may be that we cannot be as specific as we might like concerning what the essential point of holding a polyathlon is. Perhaps there is room for honest disagreement. Perhaps the matter is conceptually underdetermined. But this much it seems we can say. Whatever it is in detail, it includes or contains as a part ("part of the point is . . .") that feature wherein it differs from the point of holding a single-event competition. And that is, of course, that the overall result depend upon the outcome of more than one event.

A similar rationale can be given for (D) in the social-choice setting. There is something peculiarly pointless about holding an election in which one person's preferences determine the outcome regardless of how all the others vote. Why hold the election at all? Why not just consult the dictator straightaway? As before, there might be some extraneous, de facto reason. Perhaps we go through the motions of printing up and distributing ballots, counting votes, and so on, to deceive our own subjects, or to mollify "world opinion," or to get the propaganda benefits of "democratic" procedures. But these are transparently beside "the point." Yet again, it is not obviously irrational to have a dictatorship: immoral, destructive of human dignity, abhorrent to liberty lovers everywhere; but not obviously irrational. If, on the other hand, one wants an acceptable *collective*-choice mechanism, then to have a dictatorial device is irrational. Dictatorship is not collective choice at all.

Requirement (P′), Pareto principle: If X defeats Y in every event without exception, X places above Y in the overall ranking.

A rationale for this is available which is similar to that just given for (D'). Appealing again to the point, or part of the point, of holding a polyathlon, it includes having the overall ranking—the decision, athletically speaking, as to who is better than whom—depend on performances in the various events. This, in turn, presumes something like this: There is something to be decided; it is not obvious how things will come out; the problem of which competitor is best all-round athlete does not just resolve itself. In short, there is something like controversy, dispute, or uncertainty, which holding the competition is a way of settling. Next, we do not just want the issue disposed of any old way, like an itch we are eager to be rid of. We want it resolved in a way that is appropriately responsive to individual performances in the separate events. No doubt the notion of being "appropriately responsive" is vague and ill defined. But it can be argued that the most appropriate, least controversial response is to implement unanimity. Any outcome other than implementation would be less responsive. Any setting other than unanimity would be potentially more controversial. That is, there is no possible way to rank the competitors in a non-unanimity setting which will be as satisfactory from the point of view of settling controversy as will some way of ranking them in a unanimity setting, namely, implementation of the unanimous rankings. So if the point (or part of the point) of holding polyathlon competitions is to settle or at least reduce a certain sort of controversiality, it does seem reasonable to require a scoring system to do this in the easiest, simplest, most clear-cut situation it can encounter. If it does not even implement unanimity—the best solution for the easiest case—what hope has it?

This rationale, such as it is, also carries over to (P) in the psychological setting. There the point (or part of the point) of holding elections is to settle disputed issues, to decide which candidate shall be chosen, or what issue implemented. And again, not just to settle the controversy, but to do so in a way that is appropriately responsive to individual preferences. Finally, only in unanimity settings is it unambiguously clear what this requires. But it is clear there. Reflecting or implementing unanimous preferences is required and nothing else will do. Hence, (P).[3]

3. There is another possible rationale for (P'), which, however, does not apply to (P), and the reason for this is interesting. Viewed from one angle, the point (or part of the point) of holding a polyathlon is to determine who is the best all-round athlete, where *ceteris paribus* the criterion of all-round-athletic-betterness is the ability to defeat an opponent in several contests requiring athletic skills. All-round-athletic-betterness, then, is a compositional matter. Its increments are victories in various polyathlon events. So if one competitor defeats another in every separate event he is, by definition, a better all-round athlete. A scoring system must certify him as such on pain of violating (part of) its *raison d'etre*. This rationale differs from the one offered previously in emphasizing not the controversiality but what the controversy is about. It does not carry over to (P) for the simple reason that there is no general notion "best all-round thing to choose" whose merit is constituted incrementally by individual choice "victories." In short, the more different events X beats Y in, the better all-round athlete he shows himself to be. But however many individuals happen to prefer X to Y, that does not tend to establish that X is *better* than Y in any interesting sense. A better vote-getter, perhaps. But the fact that that has slightly disreputable overtones is important. If we are majoritarians in the matter of social choice, we do indeed think that if X is preferred to Y by more people than otherwise, then he ought to place higher in the social ranking. But our reason for this is presumably *not* decomposible into the following inference.

The fact that more people prefer X to Y than prefer Y to X shows that X is better than Y in sense φ. If X is better than Y in sense φ, then he ought to place higher in the social ranking.

Individual preference "victories" do not testify to a kind of value that deserves rewarding by a social-choice mechanism. But individual victories in athletic events do testify to a kind of value that deserves rewarding by a scoring system. The fact that the polyathlon model has, while the social-choice setting lacks, this involvement with a regulative ideal (namely, the concept "best all-round athlete") will also be important for our examination of (I).

Some people will no doubt view (D) and (P) as intuitively obvious, self-evident evaluative judgments which require no justification at all, much less the mundane sort we offer above. We wish them well. Others, recognizing a need for justification, will nonetheless scorn as being derivative and nonbasic the type of rationale we suggest. It is true that we have, in effect, appealed to a rationality of means rather than ends. Ours is a conditional, not a categorical account. The form of our justification of (D) and (P) is:

If you want a device to do such-and-such, it is reasonable to require it to be thus-and-so.

The fact (if it is a fact) that the concept of a polyathlon, and likewise of an aggregation device or collective-choice mechanism, incorporates (in what we called its formal or essential point) the idea that we *do* want a device to do such-and-such should not obscure this. We have not attempted to show that either dictatorship or negative responsiveness is per se irrational. We have instead argued that to hold a polyathlon, and by analogy, to have a *collective*-choice mechanism or aggregation device, which infringed (D) or (P) would be. But that, of course, leaves untouched the question of whether or not to have a collective-choice mechanism at all. In short, we have not argued that it would be irrational not to hold polyathlons. Only that *if* they are to be held, then it is unreasonable for them to violate (D') or (P'). The irrationality in question is a variety of means/ends pointlessness.

(D) and (P) have, among the four requirements, the firmest foundation. They are involved, so to speak, in the very notion of reasonable collective choice itself. Things are different with (U) and (I).

Requirement (U'), unrestricted scope: Any number of events and competitors is allowed, and the competitors can finish in any order in any event.

Four Conditions on Rational Social Choice

Should we expect an acceptable scoring system to be applicable to every conceivable setting of events, competitors, and every possible way a group of competitors might finish in an event? Well, maybe it would be nice. But it does not look *pressing*. Unrestricted scope does not appear to be implicated in the very concept of holding a polyathlon, or in the point of doing same. Decathlon and pentathlon scoring systems, for instance, restrict both the number and type of events, yet do not appear to be out of court for it. Still, perhaps we can at least say this for (U'). All other things equal, greater scope is better than less. Unrestricted scope, the upper bound, has in its favor considerations of generality and simplicity, notions that have considerable intellectual appeal. Thus, although (U') cannot be considered a condition of rationality, there is a certain presumption in its favor. It can be overridden, but not for no reason, on whim. There is, as philosophers (following lawyers) say, a defeasible presumption in its favor. So (U') might be considered, in some suitably attenuated sense, a reasonable requirement. It concerns a prima facie desirable feature, and in the absence of reasons to the contrary, it is reasonable to pursue desirable ends.

There are two main varieties of restriction envisaged in (U'), numerosity restrictions and pattern restrictions. Of the two, only the latter is serious. As we remarked earlier, all that Arrow's proof requires is at least three events and three competitors. Hence, to evade the result by limiting numerosity would require such severe strictures—not permitting a scoring system to be applied to more than either two events or two competitors or both—and correspondingly strong reasons for overriding the presumption against limits, as not to be worth pursuing here. Pattern restrictions are another matter. At the heart of Arrow's proof is the *cyclical majorities* preference pattern, also known as the *paradox of voting*. This striking phenomenon was discovered in 1785 by the French mathematician and social scientist, the Marquis de

Condorcet.[4] It has puzzled and intrigued researchers ever since. Patrick Suppes explains it as follows.

The naive idea is that the method of majority decision is always fair. The counterexample known as the *paradox of voting* shatters this illusion. Let the issues be *A, B, C,* and let the group consist of three persons. The first person ranks them *ABC*; the second, *CAB*; the third, *BCA*. If the voting begins by considering *A* against *B, C* will be decided on; if it begins by considering *A* against *C, B* will win; and if it begins with *B* against *C, A* will win. In other words, which issue wins depends entirely on the order in which they come up for voting. This paradox is at the heart of all the recent economic literature on the existence of rational social decision procedures.[5]

Letting voters head rows across which are displayed the issues, with *being to the left of* representing *being preferred to*, we have this:

$$
\begin{array}{cccc}
V_1: & A & B & C \\
V_2: & C & A & B \\
V_3: & B & C & A
\end{array}
$$

A majority of voters favor *A* over *B,* a majority prefers *B* to *C,* and a majority prefers *C* to *A.* A majoritarian aggregation device therefore will generate a cyclical output: *A* socially preferred to *B, B* to *C,* and *C* to *A.*

It turns out that Arrow's result can be evaded by disallowing this particular preference pattern. Of course, to allow a device to

---

4. See Duncan Black, *The Theory of Committees and Elections* (Cambridge: Cambridge University Press, 1958), especially part 2, for a fascinating account of the history of these matters.

5. Patrick Suppes, "Problem Analysis and Ordinary Language," *Proceedings of the XIIth International Congress of Philosophy,* 1960, p. 335.

process any otherwise coherent set of individual preference schedules except when they happen to constitute a cyclical majorities pattern seems a fairly ad hoc way of proceeding. This particular pattern restriction would appear to be motivated entirely by a desire to evade Arrow's result. In the current discussion, though, we are considering only *independent* reasons for and against the four Arrow requirements. So this motivation does not here constitute grounds for overriding the standing presumption that (U') expresses.

There are other pattern restrictions, not framed explicitly in terms of barring cyclical majorities but (happily) having that as a consequence, which may seem to be less ad hoc. Among these are the *value restrictions*, of which D. Black's single-peakedness is perhaps best known.[6] One way of characterizing it is this: A group of preference rankings is single-peaked if there is some one of the choice alternatives concerning which all the voters agree that it is not worst. This can be illustrated by a situation in which the candidates or issues line up along the standard liberal/conservative spectrum. Suppose that there are three candidates, one leftist (L), one centrist (C), and one rightist (R). Single-peakedness means that the electorate view these candidates in the "reasonable" manner, each voter ranking them according to their "distance" from his favorite. Thus, left-of-center voters rank them L, C, R. Right-leaning voters rank them R, C, L. Centrist voters prefer C to the other two. Notice that in the situation described, the voters do not docilely all agree. There is "fruitful" competition between left and right, with the centrists exerting a moderating influence. Still, they all do agree that candidate C is not worst. There is no voter, for example, whose first

6. Black, *The Theory of Committees and Elections*. Black uses a geometrical method of presentation and characterization; hence the name. See also Sen, *Collective Choice and Social Welfare*, sec. 10.3, "Restricted Preferences."

choice is R, but if he cannot have R would prefer L to C; no one, that is, who prefers both extremes to the middle. Such a voter, whatever his reasons, would not rank the candidates according to their relative distance from his favorite along the liberal/conservative spectrum. A glance at the cyclical majorities pattern in the paradox of voting shows that no such special, limited agreement obtains there. Each alternative therein takes its turn at occupying the bottom of someone's list. Hence, a restriction to single-peakedness has as a consequence the barring of cyclical majorities patterns. But is it reasonable to infringe (U) in favor of a single-peakedness pattern restriction? Is there anything independently to be said on behalf of single-peakedness, other than that it has a consequence that evades Arrow's proof?

In the athletic model there does not appear to be much to say for it. There is, in general, little reason to expect that among any three athletes and events there will always (or even, often) be one competitor who will not finish last in any of the events. Of course, if a polyathlon is composed exclusively of events success in which involves two distinct abilities (for example, speed and strength) for which there is a natural trade-off, then it might satisfy the athletic analogue of single-peakedness. That is, suppose that in each event either speed beat strength (as in the dashes) or strength beat speed (as in weight lifting). Further suppose that speed and strength were inversely correlated in a continual trade-off. The stronger one is, the slower; and the faster, the weaker. Now consider three athletes, A, B, C, such that A is very strong but very slow; C is very fast but quite weak; and B is moderately strong and moderately fast. Plausibly, B would never lose. In strength events he would beat C and get beaten by A, and in speed events he would beat A and get beaten by C. And, by hypothesis, there are only strength and speed events in this polyathlon. So, B never comes in last. That is, all events in such a polyathlon "agree" about one competitor, namely B, that he does not finish last. This is single-peakedness, but hardly typical.

Four Conditions on Rational Social Choice

In the social-choice (psychological) arena there is perhaps a bit more plausibility to the claim that single-peakedness often does obtain. For some electorates, at any rate, issues or candidates do fall naturally onto an appropriate continuum, the liberal/conservative spectrum being one such. There most voters might indeed tend to rank candidates by their relative distances from their preferred positions on that scale, and hence agree about some candidate (namely, the centrist) that he is not worst. And so their preferences would not, in fact, fall into a cyclical majorities pattern.

But these considerations do not seem to provide independent, positive grounds for breaching (U) in favor of a single-peakedness restriction; grounds, that is, exclusive of the motivation to evade Arrow's result. They perhaps show that if there were *other* (independent) positive grounds for doing so, then the costs would not be as great as might be expected. There is a sense in which, on practical grounds, forswearing certain sorts of preference patterns is less objectionable than it otherwise would be, to the extent that those forsworn patterns are less likely to occur anyhow. But having less bad to be said against a thing than might have been expected is not the same as having anything at all good to say in its favor. Suppose, contrary to fact, that there was reason to think that single-peakedness did characterize many polyathlons. Would that provide positive reason for infringing the standing presumption in favor of generality? For inhibiting our scoring system's capacity to process statistically aberrant settings? It seems not. If they do not occur very often, and even if we see why they do not, that does not provide good reason not to be able to handle them when they do. Perhaps if it could be shown that cyclical majorities patterns were impossible (not just unlikely, or de facto nonexistent), then the generality presumption would lapse. (It is usually held no restriction on God's omnipotence to be unable to accomplish the impossible.) But even here, this is a case of the standing presumption *lapsing*, not of our finding positive grounds to override it. Besides, cyclical majorities are not impossible.

(U') then, and by analogy (U) in the psychological setting, is not implicated in the very concept of (the point of) holding a polyathlon (using an aggregation device). It is, instead, a defeasible requirement of desirability, based on a standing presumption in favor of generality. As such, it is more vulnerable to the possibility of reasonable infringement than either (D') or (P').

Requirement (I'), the independence of irrelevant alternatives: The overall ranking of any given set of competitors depends only on the order of finish of those competitors.

There is no hope of making (I') out to be implicated in the concept of (the point of holding) a polyathlon, as a moment's thought will disclose. Can we then even show it to be, like (U'), a defeasible requirement of desirability—a feature which, all other things equal, it would be better to have in a scoring system than not, provided that there were no overriding reasons to the contrary?

Since (I') is framed in terms of any group of competitors, it holds for any pair (a pair being a group). The relative positions of any two athletes in the overall rankings, then, must depend only on the relative order of finish of those two athletes (in each event). Notice what this requires and what it rules out. First, it requires that the only information allowed to count will be information concerning order of finish in the separate events. The scoring system is not permitted to respond to any margin of victory (intensity of defeat) information: neither differences in heights cleared (in jumps), distances covered (in throws), nor time elapsed (in runs). Nor to other information that might seem relevant, like total number of attempts (in jumps and vaults) or number of hurdles struck.[7] Nor, for that matter, can it respond to

7. Except, of course, where such matters figure in determining or-

31

age and size of competitors (as a basis for handicapping in races, or, as in boxing and wrestling, weight classifications), relative amounts of energy expended or pain tolerated—supposing that measurable—grace and style, and so forth. Only order of finish: this one ahead of that one, those two tied. We shall call this the *ordering* or *ordinality* aspect of (I′).

Second, (I′) requires that in ranking any two competitors, the scoring system not be sensitive to information concerning any other competitor. In view of the first (ordering) aspect, this means information concerning how any other competitor "places" vis-à-vis one or the other or both of the two in question, or any other competitor(s) for that matter. So, for example, the scoring system cannot take into account, in its ranking of X and Y, the (possible) fact that although X beat Y in the high jump and shot put, Y beat Z, W, U, V (all of whom beat X), *and* X in the 100-meter dash and pole vault. Information about these other competitors is not allowed to influence the ranking of X and Y. We shall call this the *independence* aspect of (I′).

One effect of this condition is worth noting. It guarantees that the overall ranking of any given-sized group of competitors is always decomposible into (or, viewing matters from the other direction, built up out of) successive pairwise comparisons. Suppose that a scoring system ranks seven athletes on the basis of their performances in a polyathlon. Then let one of the seven be disqualified. Nothing else has changed, the races are over and done, the order-of-finish information for each event is recorded. The data, in short, for the surviving six competitors (vis-à-vis each other) remain exactly what they were before the seventh was disqualified. Suppose then that the scoring system is applied

---

der of finish in the individual events. (I′) prohibits them from affecting the aggregation itself, not the individual inputs which get aggregated. So, in actual practice, ties in the high jump and pole vault are resolved (where possible) on the basis of fewest total attempts.

to these (unchanged) data concerning the six. If it satisfies (I'), it must rank the surviving six in exactly the same positions (relative to each other) that they occupied in the original ranking of seven. If not, if it fails to preserve the original outcome, then its ranking of the six must have depended in part on the presence of the seventh. By hypothesis, that is the only feature of the situation that has changed. Then its ranking did not depend *only* on the relative order of finish of the six. (I') prohibits the ranking of any group from depending on information concerning any competitor not in the group. Successive repetitions of this reasoning result in ultimate rankings of pairs, which must be what they are regardless of the size group they are embedded in. Hence, pairwise choice.

Now we are in a position to see what can be said for and against (I'). Take the second, independence, aspect first. A scoring system that violates this part of the (I') requirement is the rank-order system, which works as follows. To the n various places of finish in an event, it assigns fixed numerical weightings (scores): n points for first place, $n - 1$ for second, $n - 2$ for third, and so on. Having awarded points to each contestant in each event, according as he places in that event, the system totals up these points across the whole polyathlon and generates an overall ranking based on the relative sizes of the totals. The more total points a contestant has, the higher he places in the overall rankings.

Suppose now that we have a polyathlon, call it M, containing three events, A, B, C, and four competitors, X, Y, Z, W, with order of finish for events A and B: X, Y, Z, W, and for event C: Z, W, X, Y. The rank-order system awards 10 (total) points to X, 8 to Z, 7 to Y, and 5 to W. Its overall ranking from M, then, is X, Z, Y, W. Now consider the polyathlon M^*, derived from M by deleting (disqualifying) competitor Y, all else unchanged. In M^* the order of finish for events A and B is X, Z, W and for event C it is Z, W, X. This is the same relative order of finish for each event that

33

these three competitors had in M. When applied to M^* the rank-order system awards 7 (total) points to X, 7 to Z, and 4 to W. The overall ranking from M^*, then, is $(X = Z)$, $> W$.[8]

Since the relative positions of X and Z in the overall standings get changed—from X defeating Z in M, to Z tying X in M^*—as a result only of the deletion of competitor Y, the rank-order system is not independent of irrelevant alternatives. It violates the second (independence) aspect of (I'). For competitors X and Z it was the presence or absence of Y, not just their relative order of finish vis-à-vis each other in every event, which made a difference to their overall standing. That is, X suffered in the overall rankings vis-à-vis Z, he went from defeating to merely tying him, solely as a result of the disqualification of Y (whom he beat in every event).

Regarding the alleged unacceptability of this outcome, people's intuitions appear to vary. Is such a possibility always to be avoided? And if so, at what cost? Some feel that to allow it would be unfair or unjust. This is presumably on grounds that a competitor's overall standing could be altered even though he stood (rel-

---

8. This is an adaptation of an example used by Arrow in *Social Choice and Individual Values*, p. 27. In tabular format:

	Event	Places					Points Awarded			
		1st	2nd	3rd	4th		X	Y	Z	W
	A	X	Y	Z	W		4	3	2	1
M	B	X	Y	Z	W		4	3	2	1
	C	Z	W	X	Y		2	1	4	3

Totals: 10 7 8 5
Overall ranking: X, Z, Y, W

	Event	1st	2nd	3rd			X		Z	W
	A	X	Z	W			3		2	1
M*	B	X	Z	W			3		2	1
	C	Z	W	X			1		3	2

Totals: 7 7 4
Overall ranking: $(X = Z)$, W

34

ative to the remaining others) the same as before in each separate event. Thus, he might suffer or benefit, not through any effort or accomplishment on his (or their) part, but merely through the machinations of the scoring system. This is hardly being rewarded or penalized according to one's deserts, and hence by many lights, unfair. Perhaps this makes violations of this aspect of (I') objectionable in some sense, but hardly irrational. A great deal depends on what possible benefits there are in allowing such violations. It might turn out, for instance, that the simplicity, ease of administration, apparent widespread acceptance, and so forth, of rank-order systems compensate for such occasional anomalies. There are, of course, sterner souls who say, "Let justice be done though the heavens fall!" But there are others who say, "We must count the costs; weigh and balance." The matter appears to be controversial. Perhaps there does stand behind the independence aspect of (I') some principle of giving a competitor his just deserts. And perhaps that is enough to create a weak presumption in its favor. After all, when we raise the question of whether the rank-order system might not have compensating advantages, we assume that there is something bad about it that needs compensating for.

Anyhow, this rationale, such as it is, appears to carry over to the independence aspect of (I) in the social-choice setting. Rank-order voting is not unusual, especially as an aggregation device for small groups. Often it is used to establish a set of priorities for such a group—college faculty, church vestry, union steering committee—"democratically." A list of possible goals or aims is drawn up and submitted to the membership for each to rank in order of his preference. Numbers are then assigned to each voter's rank ordering in the prescribed manner: n points for first choice, $n - 1$ for second, and so on. Totals are calculated for each choice option and the community's priority ranking derived from the relative sizes of these sums. In a certain sense this amounts to squeezing cardinal blood out of an ordinal turnip.

The connecting link is the (hazardous?) assumption that the numbers assigned to the various preference "ranks" give approximate preference intensity measures. (Arbitrary though such a uniform assignment may seem to be, what else can those numbers be doing?) The inherent possibility of some option benefiting or suffering "through no fault of its own," through addition or deletion of other options, is equally present here as in the athletic scoring case.

In shielding the social ranking of any pair from the "outside influence" of "irrelevant alternatives," this second, independence aspect of (I) thereby prohibits strategic manipulation: the deliberate exploiting of such anomalies to gain some candidate (or, competitor) advantage. A familiar manifestation of this in the political arena is the employment of stalking horses. Think, for example (in a reversal of the recent rank-order voting case), of X's wily campaign manager, realizing that his candidate will not defeat Z if only he, Z, and W run, inducing Y to join the race. One's sense of unfairness is perhaps heightened by the element of deliberate manipulation, but the objection seems at bottom the same: a candidate benefits (or, suffers) vis-à-vis another through no merit (or fault) of its own.

The other part of (I'), the ordinality aspect, is in a different position concerning independent justification from anything we have examined so far. Unlike (D') and (P'), it is not arguably connected with the concept of (the point of) holding a polyathlon. Nor like (U')—and perhaps also the independence aspect of (I')—does it appear to be a defeasible requirement of desirability, with a standing presumption in its favor which at least requires good reason to override.

What can be said for it? Why should a scoring system be restricted to information concerning only order of finish? There appear to be two main possible sorts of answers:

(1) It might be thought that no further information can be reliably ascertained, or

(2) It might be thought that, even if it could be reliably had, it should not be used.

This latter possibility divides into two main subcases:

(a) Using such further information might have various unwanted side effects, and
(b) The famous difficulty of making interevent comparisons.

Take (1) first. There can certainly be situations in which a restriction to ordinality is reasonable because nothing else is available. Imagine a polyathlon comprising several long-distance foot races, taking place without benefit of timers of any sort—clocks, hourglasses, burning wicks, or whatever. Let each event be laid out across a winding, hilly, one-way course, precluding lap counting or a view of more than one contestant at a time at the finish line. Since under these conditions only order-of-finish information could be reliably obtained, it would be reasonable to restrict oneself to it. But these are fairly specialized circumstances. They certainly have nothing to do with the idea of aggregating the results from separate events into an overall ranking per se. In fact, it *is* often possible to ascertain "stronger" relevant information than mere order of finish. Chronometers and various other measuring devices provide reasonably accurate, objective information concerning margin of victory. And if it can be had, why not use it? Indeed, it could be argued that, just as the separate ordinal victories constitute increments toward "overall athletic betterness," even more so does size of victory margin. If X is, *ceteris paribus*, better than Y for defeating him, he is that much better, it would seem, for beating him badly. Hence, the very point of holding polyathlons—to determine who is best all-round athlete—would appear to dictate using such information if it could be had, rather than forswearing it as (I') requires.

Four Conditions on Rational Social Choice

With regard to (1), the issue of reliable obtainability, (I')
seems to be derivative from a more general precept:

(G'): Use only such information as can be reliably obtained!

This, together with the subsidiary factual claim,

(F'): Only order-of-finish information can be reliably obtained.

yields[9] the ordinality aspect of (I'),

Use only order-of-finish information!

Since the subsidiary factual claim (F') is false, this aspect of (I')
would appear to be unsupported. It goes without saying that the
analogous factual claim for the social-choice setting is much
more controversial. It states that only order-of-preference information can be reliably obtained. But false through it may be, it is
not as obviously false as is its athletic counterpart.

General injunction (G') does seem to pertain to the rationality
of aggregation mechanisms. But its plausibility is quite independent of the subsidiary factual claim concerning what sort of information can be reliably had. If all that can be had is order-of-
finish information, then the system should not be designed to respond to how badly one contestant beats another, that is, to
margin of victory, or intensity of defeat. If both order of finish
and margin of victory can be reliably ascertained, but not, say,
relative amounts of effort expended, then the system should respond only to the former two and not to the latter. If all three of
these, but not grace and style, then similarly. Furthermore, not
only does the ordinality requirement serve to rule out further rel-

---

9. Not only is this a naked and unashamed appeal to the intuitions
that ground imperative logic, but the sort of analysis here displayed—the
"factoring out" of various strands of rational support backing up a particular controversial injunction—constitutes one of the best arguments
for the need for, and existence of, imperative inference.

evant information (which would be good to have, but unfortunately cannot be reliably obtained), it also rules out irrelevant information such as astrological data, color of hair and eyes, and so forth. But this is again independent of what particular level of relevant information is reliably obtainable. It has nothing to do with ordinality as such. We would presumably want it done whatever sort of relevant information was judged to be reliably obtainable.

Summing up this part of our discussion, any plausibility the ordinality aspect of (I') has is probably due to a more general injunction that underlies it, namely, that a scoring system should respond only to relevant information that is reliably obtainable. Even though the factual premise required to translate this into the details of (I') is false—order of finish is not the only relevant information reliably obtainable—the general injunction appears to be a reasonable constraint to place on a scoring system.

We have now examined one of the possible grounds for requiring ordinality *in our athletic model*—that no information other than order of finish is both relevant and reliably obtainable—and found it wanting. There remains the other, namely, that even if it can be reliably had and is relevant, still, we should not use stronger-than-ordinal information. This we divided into two possibilities: (a) possible unwanted side effects of using such information, and (b) the problem of making interevent comparisons. In connection with (a), let us focus on margin-of-victory, or intensity-of-defeat, information. This appears to be relevant and reliably obtainable. It may, as was previously suggested, be connected to the very concept of all-round athletic betterness. And we can certainly find out, for example, not only that X beat Y and Z beat W in the pole vault, but that the amount by which X beat Y was (much) greater than that by which Z beat W. In fact, we can measure this with all desired accuracy and objectivity.

But now suppose it should turn out that large victory margins are not just randomly distributed across events. Suppose, that is, that some events appear "naturally" to dictate a greater spread among their contestants than do others. Then a system that weights in favor of victory margin (in addition to mere order of finish) will have the effect of counting results from these events more heavily in the overall rankings than it does results from other events. This discrimination among events may not seem much of a consideration against responding to margin-of-victory information. Indeed, some would argue that it is a reason in favor of doing so. (Such events might be thought to be just the ones that "separate the men from the boys," and hence *deserve* to have more influence in the determination of athletic betterness.) But the comparable situation in the social-choice setting is a different matter. There, taking account of preference intensities (in addition to mere preference orders) has the effect of favoring fanatics over moderates, which some people find objectionable. At any rate, this is an example of an unwanted side effect; an argument to show that even if we could get intensity information we should not use it. And hence, if sound, it provides some kind of support for the ordinality aspect of (I').

Point (b), the problem of interevent comparability, is as follows. Suppose that using margin-of-victory (intensity-of-defeat) information has no such unwanted side effects. Or if it has them, that they are outweighed by the intrinsic desirability of its use. And suppose that it is judged both relevant and reliably obtainable. The problem is that there does not appear to be any nonarbitrary way to aggregate such diverse types of data. In a favorite phrase, it is like adding apples and oranges. Suppose we get the information that X beat Y by 10 seconds in the 1600-meter run, while Y beat X by 3 centimeters in the high jump and by 7 meters in the javelin throw. What do we do with those numbers? Add, subtract, multiply, or divide? A victory margin of 3 centimeters in the pole vault is worth how many tenths of a second in the hurdles? It is not that we cannot answer such questions at all. The actual scoring of decathlons and pentathlons, for example, accepts the arbitrariness and gets on with it. It is that we are tempted by what might be called a principle of insufficient reason. When you don't have a nonarbitrary way to do a thing, don't do it at all. This is, of course, a nonabsolute, defeasible affair. It can be overridden. But it is a consideration which, all else equal, tends to support ordinality against cardinality.

How much of this discussion of the ordinality aspect of (I') carries over from the athletic to the social-choice setting?

(1) As regards obtainability, the issue is the same. Is order of preference the only relevant information reliably obtainable or is it not? The general principle that we factored out—Use only relevant information that is reliably obtainable!—seems as reasonable here as it was there. But the implicit subsidiary factual claim is much more controversial. We will not attempt to answer that very large, substantive question just now. Instead, we will settle for a conditional result. If order of preference turns out to be the only relevant information reliably obtainable, then (I) is strongly supported by the general principle adverted to above. If however, there is other, stronger information, both relevant and reliably obtainable, then (I) receives no support at all from this principle, however it fares on other grounds.

(2) Aside from obtainability, what else can be said for and against the ordering aspect of (I)? Even supposing that we could get stronger information than mere preference orderings, should we use it or not? Are there independent reasons for restricting ourselves to ordinal data in the manner prescribed by (I)?

The question we shall pursue first is whether there are any unwanted side effects of using such further information. If there are, perhaps they will be severe enough to outweigh whatever prima facie desirability its use has. This would provide grounds for keeping hands off it even if it were available. As a beginning, let us return to a point previously mentioned. In the preceding discussion, we framed our "factored-out" general principle in terms of the notion of relevance. This was to reflect the fact that (I) not only rules out relevant but ungettable, but gettable and irrelevant, information. In the polyathlon model this was all quite straightforward. Margin-of-victory information was prima facie relevant. Contestant hair and eye-color information was not. The one is, but the other is not, relevant to the question of who is best all-round athlete. Questions of relevance in the polyathlon model are settled by reference to a guiding, regulative concept, namely, the notion "all-round athletic betterness." For any given factor, if it makes for all-round athletic betterness, it is relevant. If it doesn't, it is not.

But what decides such questions in the social-choice setting? There is no guiding, or regulative, concept, "best all-round thing to choose" for relevance to be decided by. In the athletic setting, we can see the plausibility of saying, "*Ceteris paribus*, one athlete is better than another for achieving an equivalent standard with less expenditure of effort, while tolerating a greater amount of pain, at a greater age, and so forth." We can see how to extend the list. We know what sorts of considerations bear on including an item or not. In the social-choice setting, on the other hand, there is order of preference, intensity of preference, and *what*? For that matter, what is to be said for taking preference intensity into account even if it could be reliably ascertained? Why is it even prima facie relevant to social choice?

The point is, for the social-choice setting, it is not even clear what further information, beyond order of preference, would be nice to have if only we could get it. Historically, of course, the main contender has always been preference intensity. Majoritarian democrats have traditionally been taunted with the situation of 51 percent mildly for, 49 percent violently against.[10]

10. See, for example, Nicholas Rescher, *Introduction to Value*

Whatever appeal this thought experiment has to our anti-majoritarian sentiments, it surely carries the assumption that preference-intensity information is relevant for social choice and deserves to be taken into account.[11] But, of course, the question is not: Do many people unreflectively assume that preference intensities are relevant? The question is: What, if anything, is it about preference intensities that makes them relevant?[12]

Suppose that for some reason it has been decided to consult individuals' preferences in arriving at a collective choice. Why should it be thought desirable (if feasible) to weight these preferences according to intensity? A number of possible reasons suggest themselves, none of them terribly compelling. For instance, there is the hedonistic utilitarian approach.

Theory (Englewood Cliffs, N.J.: Prentice-Hall, 1969), p. 69, where, speaking of a preference-intensity illustration, the author says in a footnote: "This crude machinery is, for example, sufficient to exhibit the inadequacy of settling the matter of socially preferential choice by voting. For consider the case of such a choice between two alternatives, X_1 and X_2, where a majority would grade both X_1 and X_2 as neutral, but have a slight preference for X_1 over X_2, whereas a sizable minority grades X_2 as perfectly wonderful and X_1 as absolutely ghastly, and views the difference between them as a virtually life-and-death issue."

11. This must be distinguished from the appeal of such emotively laden terms as "tyranny of the majority," which assume that some things ought not be put to a vote at all. That is, some issues, such as "fundamental rights" and other good things, deserve special treatment and are not up for ordinary methods of social-choice determination. Usually, when people speak of the tyranny of the majority, they do not have in mind alleged abuses that could be corrected, or even ameliorated, by weighting for preference intensities. That would merely trade tyranny of the majority for tyranny of the (fanatical) minority.

12. Or is it? It might be said that the conviction that preference intensities ought to count is not in need of further justification. It is part of the bedrock ethical data that any theory must take as a starting point. Those who can live with that sort of intuitionism are invited to omit the next bit of the discussion.

The more intense the desire, the more pleasant its satisfaction and the more painful its frustration. We have an underived obligation to maximize pleasure and minimize pain. Hence, preference intensities are relevant to social choice and should be taken into account if available.

The arguments against ethical hedonism are well known and do not need to be repeated here. Suffice it to say that a significant body of "informed" opinion denies that we have any such obligation, derived or not. The matter is at least controversial.

The argument from social stability—that it is dangerous to society to frustrate intense minorities—appears to be rather neatly balanced off by the backlash phenomenon. Mild majorities eventually get fed up with (what they perceive to be) their being pushed around by said intense minorities, reacting in ways that equally threaten social stability. The matter appears to be a draw, not clearly compelling either way, again controversial.

Some are no doubt tempted by sympathetic projection, considering how they would feel in the other fellow's shoes. Thus, they might think:

I, a member of the majority on *this* issue, would be happy to give way now—after all, I don't feel all that strongly about it—if I could be guaranteed that when I am in the minority on an issue about which I *do* feel strongly, I could have my way.

Then they might think that this last bit of ratiocination is so reasonable—appealing after all, only to enlightened self-interest—that everybody else would surely subscribe to it, too. Hence, all that remains is to sign people up for the social contract that implements the whole happy arrangement.[13] Unfortu-

13. This can be put in more up-to-date language: for example, choices made from behind veils of ignorance; social institutions designed by those who cannot foresee what position they will occupy; and so forth.

nately, upon reflection it appears unlikely that we will get evaluative rabbits out of conceptual hats. As Plato (perhaps unwittingly) showed, the road from self-interest to public concern does not go there.

Actually, what is more intriguing about this last case than its controversial conclusion—"therefore, we should take preference intensities into account"—is a psychological point that it hints at in passing. This is that there is a difference between primitive, first-order, object-directed desires, and the second-level desire to have one's way. The distinction between types or levels of desire (preferences), explored extensively in the eighteenth century by Bishop Butler (in his *Fifteen Sermons Preached at the Rolls Chapel*), opens up interesting possibilities. For instance, it is presumably possible for a person to have, overlaid upon relatively mild first-order preferences, a strong second-level preference for having his way. Now suppose that the level of intensity of one's first-order preferences is to some extent automanipulable, by various of the modern techniques of psychological judo. Then people, knowing that intense preferences are catered to in social choice, will have considerable incentive to employ these techniques upon themselves, and jack up their first-order intensity levels in order to get their way. Like game-theoretic strategy considerations (which involve misrepresenting one's real preferences to one's advantage), this *changing* of one's preference intensities to one's advantage is objectionable on its face. It involves unfairly exploiting the social-choice machinery, taking advantage of it in ways neither orginally foreseen nor intended. And, of course, it is opening the device up to preference intensities that makes this possible.[14]

14. It might be thought that if preference intensities are automanipulable, then so are preference orderings. That is, if, preferring X to Y, a man can by taking thought increase the intensity of his preference (using biofeedback techniques perhaps), then, likewise, being indiffer-

Perhaps though, talk of automanipulation of preference intensities is somewhat farfetched. Still, catering to intense preferences might produce undesirable long-range social consequences. Because what we cannot do for (or to) ourselves immediately, natural selection can do for us, in the long run. One evolutionary impact of social-choice mechanisms that cater to preference intensity would appear to be to select in favor of fanaticism. The intense shall inherit the earth. Now not only does it appear questionably fair to give the edge to fanatics over moderates anyhow, but the long-range effects of so doing surely threaten social stability.

This discussion has been somewhat inconclusive. An argument that would be decisive has this format: Any reason there can be for consulting people's preferences at all entails using preference-intensity information if you can get it.[15] An argument

---

ent between W and Z, he can presumably bring himself to prefer one to the other. (In fact, whether either can be done is an empirical question, and from the fact that one can nothing follows about the other; but let's suppose they both can.) Then it might be claimed that if the former possibility is an argument against taking account of preference intensities, the latter is equally an argument against considering preference orderings. But although the automanipulability would be there, the incentive to use it would be lacking. This interesting suggestion is due to Max Deutscher.

15. Cf. J. Rothenberg, *The Measurement of Social Welfare* (Englewood Cliffs, N.J.: Prentice-Hall, 1961), p. 139. "Assuming that we can 'measure' preference intensities with a tolerable degree of precision, is this the kind of factor which we *ought* to treat on a par with preference ordering in the context of social choice? My own opinion is that preference intensity is logically part of the very same description of individual values that includes preference order, and that if the experimental means exists to make it measureable, failure to use it constitutes an unjustifiable restriction on the validity of the schematization of social choice. . . . The case is even stronger than these general remarks would indicate. The inclusion of preference intensities may well be *prescribed* by the incorporation of value judgments already accepted in the schema."

like this would do the trick all right, but it is pretty hard to come by. What is needed is a connection between using preference orders and using preference intensities, *whatever reason* one might have for using preference orders. A somewhat easier thing to establish might be, not that general connection, but rather this: φ is *the reason* for using preference orders, and φ is also *a reason* for using preference intensity. Thus, you do not need to establish the connection for any possible reason, only for reason φ. But this argument takes on the additional burden of establishing that φ *is* the reason for aggregating individual preferences into social choice in the first place. And this is bound to be controversial. Some will say that the autonomy and dignity of the individual demands that a person be consulted in matters affecting him. Others will offer a justification of social expedience. Still others propose a historical or ideological account. It might even be argued that the function of government is to serve the interests of the governed, and that the concept of looking after a person's interests requires taking account of his preference intensities as well as their order. Anyhow, the attractions of bypassing these controversies in favor of the first, more general, format is obvious. Failing one or the other of these though, it appears that we must conclude that even if we could get reliable preference-intensity information, it is debatable whether or not we should use it in social choice.

Finally, even if we could reliably get information about individuals' preference intensities, and were convinced that it was relevant and that there were no unwanted side effects of using it which were not outweighed by compensating advantages, the question of how to use it remains. This is the famous problem of interpersonal comparability. The difficulty is in finding a nonarbitrary way of comparing one person's preference intensities with another's. We need to be able to calibrate their different scales, so to speak. Else what sense can we attach to the notion of adding them together into aggregates, whose sizes we can then compare? Recall the famous thought experiment favoring intensities: the desperate minority versus the apathetic majority. It is natural to think of this in terms of the smaller group's preferences being in aggregate more intense than the larger group's, where that does not merely dissolve into a series of one-for-one match-ups between members of each group, such that for each member of the one group there is a (unique) member of the other whose preference is less intense. The point is rather that the *aggregate* intensity strength of the minority group exceeds that of the majority. And hence a comparison of aggregates appears to be required. Maybe there is a way to do it, and maybe not. Maybe clear thinking will show that, appearances to the contrary notwithstanding, there is no need to do it. So even if it cannot be done, it does not matter. The problem of making interpersonal comparisons is both confusing and confused. Accordingly, we postpone its discussion to a later chapter.

In concluding this somewhat cursory look at the four Arrow requirements—(D), (P), (U), and (I)—through the perspective of our polyathlon scoring model, it seems fair to say that one of them, (I), stands out as the most controversial of the lot. Hence, we shall devote a separate chapter (chapter 4) to a discussion of two important issues that we raised (but postponed) in connection with it. These are the problem of interpersonal comparisons and the task of disentangling what is plausible with regard to the independence aspect of (I) from what is not. But first, let us turn to an issue that some will think already postponed overlong: the transitivity of social preference.

3

Preference, Thresholds, and Transitivity

Another model sometimes used for investigations like ours exploits the concept of a discrimination threshold, found in perceptual psychology. The following illustrates a typical use of this model.

> Adam might consider a bundle X^0 to be at least as good as X^1 merely because he lacked the power to discriminate between the two bundles; and for similar reasons X^1 might be held to be no worse than X^2. But the preference "gap" between X^0 and X^2 might be much larger than that between X^0 and X^1, or between X^1 and X^2, so that Adam might say that X^2 is better than X^0, his rather coarse standards of calibration being able to judge *their* relative standing. The combination of two "gaps," each of which is below the individual's threshold of (preference) perception, might itself be above that threshold.[1]

But is there really such a thing as "an individual's threshold of (preference) perception?" The natural interpretation of discrimination threshold phenomena presupposes a certain duality: be-

1. Peter Newman, *The Theory of Exchange* (Englewood Cliffs, N.J.: Prentice-Hall, 1965), p. 12.

tween the way a stimulus really is and how it appears to an observer; between objective fact and subjective response. One light source really is a tiny bit brighter than another, but since that increment of illumination intensity is (though real enough) too small to be detected, the two appear equally bright to an observer. Yet string enough of these too-tiny-to-be-detected increments together and you get an augmented increment (of the same sort only larger) which *can* be detected. The typical threshold situation involves something large enough (in some dimension) to cross a threshold, which something is compounded out of things of the same sort (real, but) too small individually to do so. It is doubtful that preference has the right structure to fit this model.

In general, the perceptual relation of a thing's *not being discriminably different from* another is not transitive. Omitting all psychophysical experimentation and sticking with the familiar, most people are unable to tell the difference in sweetness between a cup of coffee with no sugar, and a cup with one sugar grain. Nor can they distinguish the sweetness difference between any two cups which differ by a single grain. Yet, by adding grains one at a time to successive cups, a very sweet cup is eventually reached which can easily be distinguished from the first one with no sugar. So *being unable to tell sweetness difference* is not transitive. One might fail to distinguish cups a and b, b and c, . . ., y and z, but not cups a and z.

The analogy is tempting. Let finding x to be sweeter than y correspond to preferring x to y, and let being unable to tell the difference in sweetness between x and y correspond to being indifferent between them. Then, *by analogy with the perceptual case*, a person might be indifferent between x and y, y and z, and z and w, but nonetheless prefer x to w. An appropriate adaptation of the coffee example appears decisive. I am indifferent between a cup without sugar and a cup with only one grain, as I am between any two cups which differ by only a single grain. But

50

I prefer a cup with no sugar to one with grains equivalent to six spoonfuls. So adjacent indifferences add up to a preference, and indifference is not transitive.

How good is the analogy? In the perceptual case it is clear what it is that is too small to be noticed, individually; and what that same thing is which, when several are taken together, can add up to something large enough to cross the discrimination threshold. In the case of subjective brightness it is those little tiny illumination-intensity differences, and for cups of coffee it is the sweetness increments contributed by the successively added grains of sugar. But what plays that role in the preference case? If the analogy is doing any work, there should be preference counterparts to these little tiny, individually unnoticeable items. But, Leibniz aside, there do not appear to be any such things: no little tiny "preferencettes" which we really have, but which because they are too small to cross our preference discrimination thresholds, go unremarked.

Preference is not enough like perception for the threshold effects model to fit comfortably. This general disanalogy between preference and perception is one reason why it is wrong to equate preferring *x* to *y* with thinking (or, judging) *x* better than *y*—another mistake embodied in the quotation with which we began. Preference is not itself relative evaluation, however often it serves as a basis for relative evaluation. Evaluation, unlike preference, does have the logical structure of perception, at least as regards the issue at hand. It makes sense to contrast something's being good (or better than something else) with my thinking or judging that it is: how it is with how it appears to be; objective fact with subjective response.[2] But there are no preference coun-

---

2. The point here concerns surface phenomena only. If ethical subjectivism is correct, this surface contour of evaluation is misleading, and its manifest objective/subjective contrast without foundation. But even if it embodies a systematic and pervasive error on this head, evaluation

terparts to any of this. Not, for instance, whether I appear (to myself) to prefer x to y versus whether I really do. Other objections apart, this would not get it right with the threshold effects model. Several small, unnoticed self-deceptions do not add up to a noticeably large piece of self-knowledge.

So for various reasons it is wrong to think of preference in terms of "subjective value,"[3] as if that were on a par with other psychophysical phenomena such as subjective brightness, loudness, and so forth. Preferring x to y is not evaluating it, or valuing it more highly, much less subjectively valuing it. Perhaps some have been confused by economists' occasional slips of saying "value" when they mean price. There is, of course, a difference between what something (really) costs and what someone may think or estimate that it costs. But price is not value, and to think (estimate, judge) that x is priced higher than y is not to prefer x to y. There is just no rescuing the (alleged) analogy between preference and perception, and hence the (alleged) nontransitivity of indifference borrows no support from analogies with threshold effects on perception.

But what of the examples themselves? Surely the cups-of-

---

does display the contrast. See J. L. Mackie, *Ethics: Inventing Right and Wrong* (New York: Penguin, 1977), chap. 1.

3. As, for example, when S. S. Stevens speaks of

a question of lively interest in a field far removed from psychophysics, but which is not unrelated to the issue of subjective measurement. It concerns the subjective value of money (or of commodities in general). Subjective value is what the economists designate by the term "utility," which they speak of measuring in subjective units called "utiles." The question is, can utility be measured in utiles the way brightness is measured in brils, or loudness is measured in sones?

in "Measurement, Psychophysics, and Utility," in C. W. Churchman and P. Ratoosh, eds., *Measurement: Definitions and Theories* (New York: Wiley, 1959), p. 46.

coffee case—adding sugar grains one at a time, remaining indifferent between successive adjacent cups, yet preferring the first to the last—surely this has a ring of plausibility to it. Perhaps it is wrongly thought of as exactly a *threshold* effect—perhaps it is merely an anomalous, emergent phenomenon—but still, it might be held, the example does not require or depend on the perceptual analogy. It is plausible in its own right, and is by itself enough to establish that indifference is not transitive.

Let us then, address transitivity directly. One fact is initially awkward. Although the cups-of-coffee case, and similar ones, appear to be counterexamples to the transitivity of indifference, there do not appear to be any similar, persuasive counterexamples to the transitivity of (strict) positive preference. This is a difference that needs explaining. Why aren't there counterexamples to the transitivity of strict preference such as there appear to be for indifference? The answer is not far to seek. Preference, like many other psychological states, is itself dependent or supervenient upon prior perceptual discrimination. In order to prefer x to y, one must first tell them apart. [The same goes for *hating* x more than y, *fearing* x more than y, *finding* x *more surprising* (*exciting, sexy, embarrassing*, and so on) than y, and many other similarly "positive" psychological states.] By contrast, being indifferent between x and y does not require prior successful discrimination. I can be indifferent between x and y either because they differ, and I tell them apart in relevant respects, but their detectable difference does not count with me; or, because whether they differ or not, I do not tell them apart in relevant respects, and so am (quite naturally) indifferent between them. Positive preference requires successful discrimination; indifference leaves the question open. [This holds equally for the "neutral" counterparts to the other "positive" states. *Not hating* (*fearing, finding surprising*, etc.) x more than y or y more than x are all compatible either with telling the difference between them but discounting it, or with not telling the difference at all.]

Preference, Thresholds, and Transitivity

All plausible counterexamples to the transitivity of indifference involve nontransitivity in the underlying perceptual discriminations. Beneath the succession of indifferences which finally add up to a positive preference is always a succession of discrimination failures that finally add up to a success. Discrimination failures are not transitive, but their counterpart successes are. If I cannot tell whether x is sweeter than y, or y than z, it does not follow that I cannot tell whether x is sweeter than z. I might be able to, or I might not. Maybe they are, in reality, equally sweet. Or maybe they feature successive, undetectably small sweetness increments which add up to detectability. But if I do detect that x is sweeter than y and y than z, then I know that x is sweeter than z. In short, from the fact that I cannot tell, it does not follow that it is not sweeter. (And so the tiny increments can add up, and a detectable difference emerge.) But from the fact that I can tell, it does follow that no emergent detectability surprises are in store.

This is why there are counterexamples to the transitivity of indifference but not to the transitivity of (strict) preference. Indifference nontransitivity is supervenient upon perceptual nontransitivity—namely, the nontransitivity of perceptual discrimination failures. But strict preference presupposes discrimination success, and there are no nontransitivities of discrimination success. Hence, there are no counterexamples to the transitivity of strict preference. Which explains why not only are there no counterexamples to the transitivity of strict preference, there are none to indifference either *when it is explicitly overlaid upon discrimination successes*. In other words, it is essential to the plausibility of the coffee-cups case that I not be able to tell the difference in sweetness between the successive cups, each of which differs by only a single sugar grain. My successive indifferences must result from these perceptual failures in order for the emergent switch from indifference to positive preference to be plausible. To rob the counterexample of its force we need only assume that I can distinguish the sweetness contribution of each successive single sugar grain. Or, avoiding fantastic hypotheses, recast the entire story in spoonfuls rather than grains. It might be thought that nothing could be easier than to have a gross preference discontinuity, a "threshold," in macro (spoonfuls) as well as in micro (grains) terms. So, I am indifferent between spoonful increments up to five, not setting much stock by sweetness anyway, but at six spoonfuls the stuff becomes sickeningly sweet and I remain no longer indifferent. However, this situation poses no threat to transitivity. The switch from indifference to preference occurs, not between zero and six (and nowhere in between), but between five and six.

The moral is that the real trouble with transitivity is not attributable either to preference or to indifference. It springs from the perceptual discriminations, or rather discrimination failures, which can underlie one but not the other. In other words, whatever nontransitivity there is in these preference relations (including now, broadly, both preference and indifference), it is dependent on prior, perceptual nontransitivities. And that sort of *dependent* nontransitivity is a fairly stale and uninteresting one. What would be exciting would be a case of preference nontransitivity overlaid upon total discrimination successes. This would locate the nontransitivity squarely with the preference (or indifference) itself, not its underlying perceptual presuppositions. But such cases are not forthcoming. Which all inclines one to make contradictory judgments about the transitivity question. Indifference is not transitive, one wants to say, as the counterexamples show. But on the other hand, it really is not the indifference itself which is shown not transitive. It is the underlying perceptual discriminations (discrimination failures, really). As usual, when we encounter a contradiction, we make a distinction.

Among the familiar properties of binary relations, in addition to transitivity, are symmetry, reflexivity, and total reflexivity.

Preference, Thresholds, and Transitivity

The distinction between the latter pair—reflexivity and total reflexivity—provides the means of resolving our apparent contradiction. A binary relation R has total reflexivity when everything has R to itself. The relation of identity, for example, is totally reflexive: everything is identical with itself. Nontotal (or ordinary) reflexivity, on the other hand, characterizes a binary relation R when *anything that stands in the R relation at all* has R to itself. The relation "being the same color as" is reflexive but not totally reflexive. Not because there are colored things that are not the same color as themselves, but because there are things that are not colored at all—like numbers and tunes —which, since they are not the same color as anything, are not the same color as themselves. Reflexivity here could be expressed in conditional form: *If* a thing has any color at all, it has the same color as itself. Usually, when it becomes a matter of controversy whether a relation is reflexive or not, the qualification (to things that stand in the relation at all) is operative but suppressed or implicit in our thinking. Thus, in denying that the "admires" relation is reflexive we do not normally say this on the ground that there are things like rocks which do not stand in the relation at all; as we might, if total reflexivity were in question. Instead, we deny it because we think of persons who, although they admire others, do not admire themselves.

We need a similar distinction between what might be called total preferential transitivity, which holds (when it does) for everything without qualification, and (chastened) preferential transitivity, which holds for things that meet a certain enabling qualification. The qualification is that the subject make the appropriate perceptual discriminations. Indifference, then, we could say is (chastenedly) transitive but not totally transitive. It is not true, as a matter of logic, that if x is indifferent to y, and y to z, then x is indifferent to z, for all individuals and all triples of alternatives. But it is true for all individuals *who make the relevant perceptual discriminations*. Just as with strict preference, there are no counterexamples to the claim that indifference is (chastenedly) transitive. As with reflexivity, so with transitivity: notwithstanding the fact that the "total" versions of these notions are much simpler to formulate, it is the "nontotal," the chastened versions, that are normally meant. Anyone who remains troubled by the alleged ideality or unreality of the typical transitivity assumption governing individual preference structures is free to insert "(chastenedly)" before each occurrence of "transitive." The loss in generality will be negligible, and he will not be vulnerable to cups of coffee refutation.

Otherwise put, the point is this. The plausible counterexamples to the transitivity of indifference do not show the whole idea completely mistaken. What they show is that under certain very limited, special conditions—conditions we can independently recognize, and whose workings we understand—transitivity breaks down. The question then becomes: Do we give up the transitivity assumption altogether, or do we modify it slightly so as to isolate and disarm the counterexamples? Prudent, conservative practice dictates the latter course. All plausible cases of indifference nontransitivity turn out to be consequential upon prior nontransitivities of perceptual discrimination. They show that where there is a certain, very special series of failures of perceptual discrimination, there nontransitivities of indifference can be expected. They do not show that, in general, there can be such nontransitivities, as reflection on the cups-of-coffee case, with spoonfuls in place of sugar grains, reveals.

Finally, when it is debated whether preference is transitive, or whether Arrow's logical well-behavedness assumption is reasonable, what is the argument really about? Is the issue "empirical" or "normative" or what? There is so much room for confusion over this that, even at the risk of committing methodology, it is worth trying to talk sense about it, if only briefly. The question of whether preference is transitive—or, more generally, the

57

question what are the logical features of the preference relations—concerns an idealization we can call *rational preference*. It asks, in effect, whether the preferences of an ideally rational preferrer would be transitive. This is not a question of empirical fact, and is thus not settled by devising tests to discover what people say or do in variously artificial choice situations. It does not matter what people actually do; what matters is whether, in doing what they do, they are departing (or not) from the ideal of rationality. What the ideal is is never determined by the facts.

This is why our previous discussion (of transitivity and cups of coffee) could proceed in terms of *plausible* counterexamples rather then actual experiments. There it was claimed that there are no plausible counterexamples to transitivity of strict preference, and likewise none to transitivity of indifference when overlaid upon discrimination successes. But suppose someone says, "Here is a counterexample: a person strictly prefers X to Y, Y to Z, and Z to X." Is that a counterexample to our earlier claim? It is certainly not a *plausible* counterexample. We never claimed that deviant preference patterns do not, or cannot, actually occur. No doubt for any concept of rationality there will be crazy people, people who are irrational according to that concept. Their behavior presents no difficulty for any given theory; unlike a plausible counterexample, which, unless explained away, wrecks a theory. Because a plausible counterexample presents not deviant behavior as fact, but deviant behavior as familiar.

Suppose that a psychologist reports encountering a subject who prefers X to Y, Y to Z, and Z to X. We ask: "Is anything special going on? Does the subject employ multiple criteria, selectively—preferring X to Y in virtue of a, Y to Z in virtue of b, and Z to X in virtue of c? Or is his attention easily distractable?" "No," we are told, "nothing special. These are the simple, unidimensional preferences of an attentive mind. He just prefers X to Y, Y to Z, and Z to X." Well then, so be it. There is no question here except the truth of the report. And that, however it turns out, has no significance for the issues we have been considering. Compare the examples of the coffee cups: (1) grain by grain, and (2) spoonful by spoonful. These are thought experiments, not real experiments. (It does not matter what would actually happen.) We test them conceptually for plausibility, not experimentally for truth. We try them on for size and check their fit. We ask: "Could I be in such a situation and (plausibly) have such preferences? Or would I have to be crazy?" Not, "Is it true?" but, "Does it ring true?"

Consider a comparable question in inductive logic. Does a person believe all the logical consequences of everything he happens to believe? If he does, then his beliefs satisfy the condition called *deductive closure*; if not, not. Now the only sensible issue here concerns the concept of *ideal rationality*. Does ideal rationality require deductive closure or not? It is plain that no actual person with a normal complement of opinions satisfies this standard. Nobody actually believes all the logical consequences of everything he happens to believe. It is equally plain that this fact is quite irrelevant. The question concerns the ideal. Does the fact that no actual person's beliefs are deductively closed constitute a defect? And if so, what sort of defect? Does it illustrate the commonplace that people are only imperfectly rational?

The answer is no, rationality does not require deductive closure. To think that it does is to confuse rationality with intelligence; to ignore the patent differences between constructing an original proof and following the explanation of a proof. Perry Mason and Kurt Gödel are not more rational than the rest of us, they are smarter. Rationality is a fairly minimal, passive recognitional affair—it involves the capacity to "see" connections, to "see" the points of things, when they are brought to our attention. It does not, like deductive closure, require the taking of any (or, any very extensive) mental initiatives. But whatever the truth about rationality here: whether it requires deductive clo-

59

sure; whether that is required by something else, not rationality; or even, as I am inclined to think, whether there is no human ideal which requires it at all—this is the same kind of issue as the question of whether preference is transitive.

Are these questions empirical? Or, normative? In fact, they are neither. They are not empirical because the facts, whatever they turn out to be, do not determine the ideal. They are not normative because they issue in no prescriptions for conduct. The "ought" of rationality is not the normative "ought." Both transitivity of preference and deductive closure of belief are subjects for discovery and description rather than invention, stipulation, or experimentation. They involve getting it right about the concept of rationality: what it requires and what it permits; and what implications that has for rational and irrational belief, behavior, and preference. This is all descriptive, if you count *conceptual* description.

4

Interpersonal Comparisons
and Noncreativity

I. Interpersonal Comparisons

We earlier separated the question of obtainability—Is there a reliable method of getting preference-intensity information on an individual by individual basis?—from the question of interpersonal comparability—How can we aggregate such information, even if we can get it? Our polyathlon scoring model is especially good at enforcing this separation because the obtainability issue there presents no difficulty at all. Of course we can get reliable margin-of-victory information—over and above order of finish—on an event-by-event basis. There are no serious issues here of observability, measurability, or, in general, empirical respectability. Yet the problem of making interevent victory-margin comparisons clearly remains. Even given that A beat B by 2.5 seconds in the 400-meter run, how does that compare with the (equally knowable) fact that B beat A by 10 centimeters in the pole vault? Or by 6 meters in the javelin throw? One of the best things about the polyathlon scoring model is its usefulness in analyzing and throwing new light on the old problem of interpersonal utility comparisons, to which we now turn.

Here is the way a decathlon is actually scored. There is an

official scoring table which displays, for each of ten events, two columns of numbers: the first represents various possible performance levels for that event (measured in appropriate units), and the second represents point-value assignments, one for each listed performance level. To find out how much a given performance (for example, an 800-centimeter broad jump) is "worth," one locates it in the performance-level column and reads across to the point-value column to see how many points are assigned a performance of that level—in this case 1020 points.[1] One can, then, consult the official scoring table and find out that a leap of so many centimeters in the broad jump is worth so many points, a run of so many seconds in the hurdles is worth so many points, a throw of so many meters in the javelin is worth so many points, and so forth. Overall rankings are calculated by adding together the total number of points awarded each contestant from all ten events, and ranking them according to relative size of totals.

This, as previously noted, constitutes a nonstandard model of a social-choice mechanism (or aggregation device). More to the point, it is a model of a device that responds to information about preference intensities, not merely to preference orderings. The results of a decathlon scoring do not just reflect contestants' order of finish in the ten events; they also reflect their respective margins of victory. Not just who beat whom, but by how much. It is the point assignments in the official scoring table, of course, which determine these interevent victory-margin comparisons. For instance, to find out how being beaten by 10.2 to 10.4 seconds in the 100-meter dash compares with being beaten by 740 to 715 centimeters in the broad jump, one looks up the point differentials in the scoring table. (In the 100-meter dash it is 1014 − 959 = 55. In the broad jump it is 901 − 850 = 51.)

1. These, and all subsequent such figures, are taken from the *Scoring Table for Men's Track and Field Events* (London: The Snow-

donia Press, International Amateur Athletic Federation, 1971), a representative page of which looks like this:

	Running events			Hurd-les	Jumping events			Throwing events		
	100 m	400 m	1.500 m	110 m						
	sec.	sec.	min.	sec.	cm	cm	cm	m	m	m
1050	-	-	3.35,3	-	223	-	499	19,69	60,57	85,80
1049	-	-	3.35,4	-	-	815	-	19,67	60,51	85,70
1048	-	45,1	3.35,5	-	-	-	-	19,65	60,45	85,61
1047	-	-	3.35,6	-	-	814	498	19,63	60,38	85,51
1046	-	-	3.35,7	-	-	-	-	19,61	60,32	85,41
1045	-	-	3.35,8	-	-	81.	497	19,60	60,26	85,32
1044	-	-	3.35,9	-	-	-	-	19,58	60,20	85,22
1043	10,1	45,2	3.36,0	-	-	812	-	19,56	60,14	85,12
1042	-	-	3.36,1	-	222	-	496	19,54	60,07	85,02
1041	-	-	3.36,2	-	-	811	-	19,52	60,01	84,93
1040	-	-	3.36,3	-	-	-	495	19,50	59,95	84,83
1039	-	-	3.36,4	13,4	-	810	-	19,48	59,89	84,73
1038	-	-	3.36,5	-	-	-	494	19,46	59,83	84,64
1037	-	45,3	3.36,6	-	-	809	-	19,44	59,76	84,54
1036	-	-	-	-	-	-	-	19,42	59,70	84,44
1035	-	-	3.36,7	-	-	808	493	19,41	59,64	84,35
1034	-	-	3.36,8	-	221	-	-	19,39	59,58	84,25
1033	-	-	3.36,9	-	-	807	492	19,37	59,52	84,15
1032	-	45,4	3.37,0	-	-	-	-	19,35	59,45	84,05
1031	-	-	3.37,1	-	-	806	491	19,33	59,39	83,96
1030	-	-	3.37,2	-	-	805	-	19,31	59,33	83,86
1029	-	-	3.37,3	-	-	-	-	19,29	59,27	83,76
1028	-	-	3.37,4	-	-	804	490	19,27	59,21	83,67
1027	-	45,5	3.37,5	-	-	-	-	19,25	59,15	83,57
1026	-	-	3.37,6	13,5	-	803	489	19,23	59,09	83,48
1025	-	-	3.37,7	-	220	-	-	19,22	59,02	83,38
1024	-	-	3.37,8	-	-	802	488	19,20	58,96	83,28
1023	-	-	3.37,9	-	-	-	-	19,18	58,90	83,19
1022	-	-	3.38,0	-	-	801	-	19,16	58,84	83,09
1021	-	45,6	3.38,1	-	-	-	487	19,14	58,78	83,00
1020	-	-	3.38,2	-	-	800	-	19,12	58,72	82,90
1019	-	-	3.38,3	-	-	-	486	19,10	58,66	82,80
1018	-	-	3.38,4	-	-	799	-	19,08	58,60	82,71
1017	-	-	3.38,5	-	219	-	485	19,06	58,54	82,61
1016	-	45,7	3.38,6	-	-	798	-	19,04	58,48	82,52
1015	-	-	3.38,7	-	-	-	-	19,03	58,41	82,42
1014	10,2	-	3.38,8	-	-	797	484	19,01	58,35	82,33
1013	-	-	3.38,9	13,6	-	-	-	18,99	58,29	82,23
1012	-	-	3.39,0	-	-	796	483	18,97	58,23	82,14
1011	-	-	3.39,1	-	-	-	-	18,95	58,17	82,05
1010	-	45,8	3.39,2	-	-	795	482	18,93	58,11	81,95
1009	-	-	3.39,3	-	218	-	-	18,91	58,05	81,85
1008	-	-	3.39,4	-	-	794	-	18,89	57,99	81,76
1007	-	-	3.39,5	-	-	-	481	18,88	57,93	81,66
1006	-	-	3.39,6	-	-	793	-	18,86	57,87	81,57
1005	-	45,9	3.39,7	-	-	-	480	18,84	57,80	81,47
1004	-	-	3.39,8	-	-	792	-	18,82	57,74	81,38
1003	-	-	3.39,9	-	-	-	479	18,80	57,68	81,28
1002	-	-	3.40,0	-	-	791	-	18,79	57,62	81,19
1001	-	-	3.40,1	-	-	-	-	18,77	57,56	81,09

Interpersonal Comparisons and Noncreativity

"How they compare with respect to what?" is a question we shall postpone. It and its social-choice counterpart raise some delicate issues best put off. Instead, we adopt a somewhat artificial, provisional answer which is at least true, however disappointing. One respect (or dimension, or feature, or property) in terms of which these victory margins can be compared is the following: the amount of impact that information about them has on the overall ranking generated by this scoring system. In the example given, they have almost equal impact—55 to 51, or 4 out of a possible 1200 points difference—with 0.2 second in the 100-meter dash getting the slight nod over 25 centimeters in the broad jump. So much for those who worry about the possibility of comparing something measured in seconds from one kind of event with something measured in centimeters from another. We prove it possible by doing it. No doubt "the amount of impact that information concerning a given item has on the overall ranking produced by some aggregation device" is not exactly the first property to spring to mind when pondering these issues of comparability. But, although complex and somewhat artificial, it *is* a property of victory margins in different events, and one in terms of which the notion of comparing them is perfectly intelligible.

But still, it might be argued—should be argued, actually, because it is true—it is not these kinds of comparisons that are at issue when the problem of interpersonal comparisons is debated. Or if it is, it is not the bare question of whether they are possible, or intelligible, or make sense at all. The heart of the problem is whether they can be nonarbitrary. The real question, in short, concerns the basis for constructing the scoring table. Certainly, these comparisons can be made once you have a scoring table, but what is the justification for the scoring table's being the way it is? And can there be an adequate justification, or is there something in the nature of things which guarantees an ineradicable element of arbitrariness?

The question, then, is not whether there is any conceivable respect whatever in which victory margins between different events can be compared. The answer to that is yes. The real issue concerns this matter of arbitrariness; which, of course, is a relative thing. Relative, not only in that it comes in degrees (more and less arbitrary) and not just absolutes (arbitrary or not); but relative to a standard or perspective or point of view. What is arbitrary from one perspective might be well-founded from another. Perhaps (but only just perhaps) there is a limiting overall concept of *total arbitrariness*, according to which a thing done or said might be arbitrary, not relative to any standard. This would be when there is absolutely nothing whatever that favors doing or saying the thing in question. Nor only nothing compelling, but nothing even relevant. An action or statement made in such splendid isolation from any of the least supporting considerations—of whatever sort, from whatever quarter, no matter how tenuous—would certainly be arbitrary. But the area of application for such a concept is vanishingly small. And, more important, one gets a distorted picture of the nature of the dispute about comparability if one frames it in terms of total arbitrariness. If one frames it that way, for example, the cardinalist is clear and easy winner: of course there is *something* to be said in favor of constructing a scoring table one way rather than another. To understand what the argument is really about, it has to be seen against a background of different conceptions of how justification should proceed. The ordinalist thinks a certain type or format of justification should be given for interevent margin-of-victory comparisons, and, failing that, they must be arbitrary. The cardinalist, having different views about what type or format of justification is required, finds *his* standards possible of attainment, and hence the resulting comparisons well grounded. Consider some of the possibilities for justifying the interevent victory-margin comparisons made by the official decathlon scoring table.

Interpersonal Comparisons and Noncreativity

First there is *indirect*, or *composite* justification, much favored by cardinalists. Its rationale is something like this. The problem is to show that certain comparisons are justified: for example, that 0.2 second in the 100-meter dash is worth slightly more, or, perhaps, four more points, than 25 centimeters in the broad jump, and likewise for all such particular comparisons made by the official scoring table. Clearly, it would be desirable not to have to justify each of these comparisons one by one, but rather to devise a general justification for the scoring table as a whole, and then observe that these particular comparisons each follow therefrom. And for this, all we need do is justify enough of the various salient features of the official scoring table to do the trick.

For instance, each of the ten events has at its disposal, so to speak, the same total "spread" of points—that is, the same absolute point distance between worst and best recognized performance levels—in this case, 1200 points.[2] This can be justified by appeal to "equal treatment of equals," or perhaps, "each event to count for one, none for more than one." To put, say, 5000 points at the disposal of the high jump while each of the other events had only 1200 would appear to constitute preferential treatment. It would allow results from the high jump more potential impact on the overall rankings than results from the others, all else equal.

Likewise, the top end of each event's scale—the best recognized performance level, the one that gets 1200 points—is set somewhat beyond the current world record for that event.[3] This not only has the practical benefit that no competitor is likely to run off the top end of the scale, but it represents another version of equal treatment. It would, after all, constitute preferential treatment for the top of all other scales to be so high while the top

2. Ibid.
3. Ibid.

of, say, the pole vault scale was set at a less demanding performance level. That would make it easier, all else equal, to get more points in the pole vault and hence give it disproportionate influence on the overall rankings.

Establishing scale bottoms—worst recognized performance levels, those which get one point—is not as simple. For jumping and throwing events there is, as it were, a natural zero, namely, takeoff or point of origin. But there is no comparable natural zero for running or hurdles events, there being no greatest amount of time it can take to traverse a given distance in a foot race. In fact, none of the natural zero points are used, even where available. The scale bottoms are most likely set by taking some average of a sampling of worst recorded performances in the various events. One supposes that there is something to be said for doing it this way.

Finally, there is the matter of point distribution: how the total 1200 points should be distributed across the recognized point-eligible spread—from worst to best performance levels—in each event. For instance, the worst recognized performance level in the broad jump is 360 centimeters, the best is 896 centimeters, for a total point-eligible spread of $896 - 360 = 536$ centimeters. The mean value per centimeter is thus $1200 \div 536 =$ approximately 2¼ points. The 1200 available points might be distributed, then, according to the following scheme. Beginning with one point for a jump of 360 centimeters, each successive performance that is 1 centimeter better than the one before gets awarded an additional 2¼ points. This scheme rates fairly well in terms of simplicity. An alternative arrangement might be this. Since incremental performance improvements up near the world record are presumably harder to come by than those any child can manage, they ought to be worth more. We might, then, follow a principle of increasing marginal returns: each successive centimeter of performance improvement gets awarded slightly more points than the last. Those near the bottom of the scale, thus, would be worth less than the average 2¼, those near the top worth more. This scheme, although a bit less simple than the previous one, is additionally supported by a version of fairness, namely, the principle that performance should be rewarded according to effort or degree of difficulty.[4]

The moral is this. If we have some kind of rationale for the total points available per event, some (possibly different) rationale for fixing tops and bottoms of scales, some (perhaps still different) rationale for point-distribution arrangements, and so forth, we are well on our way to having a composite rationale for the scoring system as a whole. And hence, in a sense, for any interevent comparison that it happens to make. Indeed, for anything else it should do. The general principle that underwrites this approach is this: Whatever is done by a (somehow) justified scoring system is itself (somehow) justified. So, appealing to simplicity here, equality there, fairness the other—with perhaps a dash of anonymity, neutrality, and other laudable things thrown in—we build up a mosaic of subjustifications, one for each of the salient constituent features of the scoring system. Of course, we never *directly* justify any particular victory-margin compari-

4. There is an interesting anomaly in the way this distribution is actually treated in the official scoring table. There, the four running-plus-hurdles events obey our second principle (of increasing marginal returns). But the remaining six jumping and throwing events obey, not either that or our first principle (of constant marginal returns), but a principle of *decreasing* marginal returns. For them, each successive increment of performance improvement is worth less than the one before; the ones near the bottom of the scale are worth more than the average and the ones near the top are worth less. In light of this remarkable peculiarity, one is tempted to draw resource management conclusions. The (scarce) resource in question is training time, and the obvious conclusion concerns the profitability (in terms of expected point production) of shifting this resource out of jumping and throwing into running and hurdling. See my "An Anomaly in Decathlon Scoring," *The Physical Educator* vol. 36, no. 1 (March 1979).

son. For instance, we never do say specifically why 0.2 second in the 100-meter dash should be worth four points more than 25 centimeters in the broad jump. Instead, we justify the system as a whole, and observe that the particular item in question follows from a justified system.[5]

In other words, the reason why 0.2 second in the 100-meter dash is held to be worth four points more than 25 centimeters in the broad jump is that when one allocates points to events in such-and-such a manner, fixes scale tops and bottoms thus-and-so, and distributes points like so, *it works out that way*. And we do have separate justifications for so designing the various constituent features of the scoring table that make it work out that way. Hence, its working out that way is not by any means arbitrary. This, then, is an example of what is meant by an indirect, composite justification.

And what is the alternative? What are the standards against which the ordinalist measures the previous rationale and finds it wanting? In short, what view of how justification *should* proceed would make it reasonable for an ordinalist to maintain, even in the face of such an indirect, composite "justification," that all interevent comparisons made by the scoring table were arbitrary? The answer is what I call the *direct, preferred* format. According to this, one should justify the claim that a given margin of victory in one event is worth more points than a given victory margin in another, by arguing directly that the one *is larger than* the other. If a scoring system is going to respond to information about margins of victory from various events, then the relative impact of such information should be based on the relative sizes of those victory margins themselves. Why else, after all,

---

5. We need a word that lacks the implication of success carried by the ordinary sense of the verb "to justify." It is controversial whether the procedure in question—the indirect or composite approach—actually constitutes (successful) justification. On this, see below.

would anybody care about victory margins rather than settling for order of finish, except from the conviction that the larger the margin of victory, the more impact it should have on the overall ranking? And if that's why you *want to* respond to it, that's how you *ought to* justify responding to it. So all this talk of simplicity, equality, fairness, anonymity, neutrality, and so forth, is quite beside the point. If the problem is to explain why, for example, getting beaten by 10.2 to 10.4 seconds in the 100-meter dash should be worth more (according to the scoring table) than getting beaten by 740 to 715 centimeters in the broad jump, the answer must be *because* a victory margin of 0.2 second (at that level) in the 100-meter dash *is larger than* a margin of 25 centimeters (at that level) in the broad jump. If such a claim either does not make sense or cannot, for some reason, be established satisfactorily, then the particular impact comparison in question cannot be justified (along the lines required by the direct, preferred format), and is (from that perspective) arbitrary.

This is a basic issue dividing ordinalists and cardinalists—although they are not always themselves too clear about it—namely, Is a direct, preferred-format justification required, or will an indirect, composite one suffice? But be that as it may, the distinction between composite and preferred-format justifications provides a handy framework for untangling and sorting out various matters which have a tendency to be run together. For example, it is possible in these terms to factor out two distinct parts of the ordinalist's objections to comparability. The first part holds that direct, preferred-format justifications are needed, and that, failing them, interevent comparisons are arbitrary. And the second part holds that direct, preferred-format justifications cannot be given. In short, we have here the classic, two-part strategy of skepticism: first argue that a certain requirement ought to be satisfied; then argue that it cannot be. Either without the other does not do the trick. The fact, supposing it to be one, that preferred-format justifications cannot be given cuts no ice if they are not anyhow required. The fact, supposing it to be one, that they are required cuts no ice if they are forthcoming. Seeing ordinalist arguments against this background makes them more intelligible, and facilitates locating where exactly various considerations actually come to bear. Similarly for the cardinalist. Does he challenge the first part, the alleged need for a preferred-format justification? Or the second, the alleged impossibility of meeting that need?

Finally, it is possible in these terms to understand the phenomenon of the cardinalist with a bad conscience. Such a person both busies himself constructing and defending indirect, composite justifications of scoring systems, and is at the same time worried about whether a direct, preferred-format justification can be given. At the least he is concerned to show that such a justification is not in principle impossible at all points. He would like, if he could, to have one clear case in which he could say, for example, that such-and-such a margin of victory in a running event is larger than such-and-such a victory margin in the pole vault, and if not support such a claim, at least understand it. And to have several of these, clearly intelligible, maybe even noncontroversial, would make him feel even better.

Now what does this amount to? Taking out an intellectual insurance policy? I do it my way, but on the outside chance that I am wrong about the main issue, I show that, even if you are right, it can still be done. Or is it possible that a composite justification can be adequate only if supplemented by a demonstration that a corresponding preferred-format justification is in principle possible? But that just seems like a failure of nerve: If it is not required, it is not required.

We will not spend a great deal of time cashing in this extended analogy, converting the whole discussion point for point into the social-choice arena. It is pretty obvious how it goes. The basic distinction between indirect, composite justifications on the one hand, and those which meet a direct, preferred-format

71

requirement on the other, survives more or less intact. For instances of the former approach, see Nicholas Rescher, *Introduction to Value Theory*,[6] app. 2, "The Social Fusion of Personal Evaluations," and almost any discussion by a cardinalist in the last thirty years in the economics literature. The usual moves are to assume numerical preference-intensity indicators given, individual by individual, and pose the problem of interpersonal comparisons as that of constructing a combination function for those number sets. Standardly, there will be developed an axiomatic characterization of said function, comprising a smallish number of axioms the glosses on which amount to subjustifications in the compositional mosaic. Sometimes the axioms are viewed as justifying the choice of one function rather than another, sometimes as exposing commitments implicit in embracing one such function. Either way it amounts to what we called an indirect or composite approach.

Assume preference-intensity information available on an individual-by-individual basis, and let the problem be to say why information about how strongly one voter prefers candidate X over candidate Y should impact more (or equally, or less) heavily on the collective choice than does information about how strongly another voter prefers Y over X. What you can bet is that you are not going to get a direct answer that shows, in the preferred-format way, that the one voter's strength of preference is *larger than* the other's. Instead, you are going to get talk about numerical and scalar manipulations, "justified" variously by appeal to notions like anonymity, neutrality, equal treatment, fairness, simplicity, and so forth, which result in a combination function according to which *it works out that way*.

Ordinalists will, as before, claim that if one person's preference intensities are to be allowed more (or equal, or less) impact

6. Englewood Cliffs, N.J.: Prentice-Hall, 1969.

on social choice than another's—in short, if they are to be "impact-comparable"—then this should be justified by showing that the one person's strength of preference is greater (or the same, or smaller) than the other's. If a social-choice mechanism is going to respond to information about preference-intensity differences from different people, then the relative impact of such information should be based on the relative size or amount of those intensity differences themselves. As before, it is catering to the *sizes* of these intensity differences which provides the *sole attraction* of the idea of responding to intensity information in the first place. If you are not going to do that, why go beyond preference orderings? And since that is why you *want to* do it, that is how you *ought to* justify doing it.

As before, the ordinalist need not claim that there is nothing at all to be said in favor of any cardinalist system. He only claims that the one required element cannot be supplied. His charge of arbitrariness, in short, is specific to his background claim that a preferred-format justification is required. Likewise, we can usefully sort cardinalist responses according as they bear on the alleged preferred-format requirement or the alleged impossibility of satisfying same, or both.

Finally, we shall discuss a couple of issues that bear on solving, rather than clarifying, the problem of interpersonal comparisons. The first concerns the matter of comparing *group* preference intensities. Using the framework previously developed, let us assume that a preferred format justification of some sort *is* required. The ordinalist claims that such a justification is impossible; the cardinalist that it is not. There are two main levels at which the dispute can occur:

(A) It is (is not) *sometimes* possible to find out about two people that one's preference for X over Y is stronger than the other's preference for Y over X.

(B) It is (is not) *sometimes* possible to find out about two *groups* of people that one group's preference for X over Y is stronger than the other group's preference for Y over X. (This assumes, of course, that it is proper to speak of the strength of a group's preference.)

Now if the ordinalist could show that it was not *ever* possible, he would have clinched his case (assuming it was required). But what about the reverse? If the cardinalist shows merely that it is sometimes possible, has he clinched his case? It might seem so, especially if one thinks that these are questions of conceivability, or what makes sense, or what is "in principle" possible. And this suggests an enormous simplification, namely, collapse the whole issue into question (A). If the question is not whether *always*, but whether *ever*, then we can argue that at least one *intergroup* comparison is "in principle" possible *if* certain *interindividual* comparisons are. And hence that (B) reduces to (A). The reasoning goes like this. Assume that it is possible to make interpersonal intensity comparisons between individuals. Now consider two groups of individuals, one consisting of eight X-choosers, the other of five Y-choosers, such that to each Y-chooser there can be paired a distinct X-chooser with preference intensity either as strong or stronger. (Each of these pairings can be accomplished by hypothesis, since none requires more than individual comparisons.) Each Y-chooser, then, is matched with an equally or more intense X-chooser, and there are three X-choosers left over, free and clear, whose preference intensities are not offset to any degree by any (otherwise unmatched) Y-chooser. Surely, however specialized the situation, it would make sense to say in this case that the one group's preference intensities exceeded the other's. And hence that the truth of (A) guaranteed the truth of (B).[7] As against this line, the following seems compelling.

7. This example, and the suggestion that "in principle" problems

If the *only* kinds of group comparisons we could make were those which fit the mold of the specialized situation described above, then what advantages would responding to preference intensities offer over simple, unweighted, ordinalistic majoritarianism? After all, if it is a case of eight to five, *X* over *Y*, why go through this elaborate matching procedure to let *X* win? In fact, there is no case in which a device, as described, would socially rank *X* above *Y*, but simple majority voting would not. And a lot cheaper, too. What is glaringly omitted, of course, is the whole class of cases that provide the motivation for wanting to respond to preference intensities in the first place: that is, cases of passionate (sizable) minorities versus apathetic (slight) majorities. To embrace cardinality in a device that cannot handle *any* of these cases is to get all its problems and none of its benefits. Yet these are exactly the cases that do not fit the specialized, one-on-one match-up mold. It is essential to the latter that the group that loses *not* be more numerous than the group that wins. Only thus can a group comparison be decomposible without remainder into repeated individual comparisons. So in order for a device to generate an intuitively attractive, nonmajoritarian outcome from these crucial-experiment situations (desperate minority, apathetic majority), it must make the sort of strong group-intensity comparison suggested in the following:

(C) It is (is not) sometimes possible to find out about two groups of people that one of them, although numerically smaller, prefers *X* to *Y* more strongly than the other, larger, group prefers *Y* to *X*.

---

with intergroup comparisons can be reduced to problems with interindividual comparisons, is taken more or less directly from R. B. Brandt, "The Interpersonal Comparison of Utility," an unpublished paper presented at the 1971 meeting of the Western Division, American Philosophical Association.

Interpersonal Comparisons and Noncreativity

The possibility of making this strong kind of group-intensity comparison is wholly untouched by any positive results concerning individual comparisons. In particular, the modern antiskeptical resolution of the problem of other minds is beside the point. Let other minds be as transparent as any behaviorist might wish; let (A) be true beyond question. Still, we are no whit the closer to showing (C) to be true.

If the only kind of group comparison whose bona fides can be established "in principle" is that which follows from the fact that individual comparisons are "in principle" possible, then let's hear no more of intense minorities and apathetic majorities. (But then, what is it all about?) On the other hand, if cardinality is to handle that problem (intense minority/apathetic majority) better than—or even, differently from—ordinality, let's see reason to think it "in principle" possible to make the strong kind of group comparison required.

What bearing does the problem of other minds have on all of this? Is it true, as is often suggested,[8] that in order to deny interpersonal comparability one has to be a skeptic about other minds? Must an ordinalist base his objection to interpersonal intensity comparisons on the grounds that nothing can be known about other minds, not even that there are any? Or, perhaps, that although some little can be known about them, it is not enough? This is not at all clear. In particular, it is unclear that the whole issue is basically epistemological, a dispute over what we can know. The comparable issue in the polyathlon setting does not seem to be *at all* epistemological. *There* there does not seem to be any serious opening for such an alleged skepticism. (The Problem of Other Events?) We know all we need to know about the existence and characteristics of the various events in a de-

8. The classic statement of this view is in I. M. D. Little, *A Critique of Welfare Economics*, 2d ed., (New York: Oxford University Press, 1957), but it is echoed in writings of Brandt, Churchman, and others.

cathlon, for instance. In particular, there is no difficulty in obtaining reliable intensity information. We can measure victory margins with all scientific objectivity, event by event. Nonetheless, there remains some difficulty in comparing, with respect to size, a victory margin of three seconds in the 400-meter dash with a margin of 3 centimeters in the high jump.

Of course, knowing (or suspecting) what is *not* at the heart of the problem of interpersonal comparisons is not as good as knowing (or suspecting) what is. But it is better than being mistaken about it. Perhaps disappointingly, we do not have a solution to the ancient and honorable problem of interpersonal comparisons. It is to be hoped, though, that our analysis of the structure of the problem, and what it does and does not involve, will make it easier for the reader to solve it for himself.

II. Noncreativity

There are two main thrusts to the independence of irrelevant alternatives: the ordinality aspect, one feature of which we just discussed at length; and the independence aspect, to which we now turn. Having seen some considerations bearing on the issue of ordinality versus cardinality, what reasons are there for or against requiring a device to be independent? For that matter, what exactly does it mean?

First, as many have noted, Arrow's choice of terminology is slightly tendentious. Whether information about certain alternatives really is irrelevant to social choice is not settled by the ordinary connotations of a piece of technical terminology. For this reason, some prefer more neutral sounding names for (I)-like requirements: independence of *extraneous* alternatives, independence of *unfeasible* alternatives. We shall continue to use Arrow's terminology, with the warning that what is called irrelevant is not thereby shown to be so.

Whatever we call them, irrelevant (unfeasible, extraneous)

alternatives are just alternatives that do not happen to be in the set from which the actual choice is being made. The commonsense notion is quite straightforward. Voters, in an election with no write-in provisions, choose among candidates listed on the ballot sheet. People (alternatives) who have not qualified for candidacy, and hence are not listed, are not available for choice. With respect to such an election, all people not listed on the ballot sheet are irrelevant (extraneous, unfeasible) alternatives. The independence aspect of (I) requires that the social ordering of any given set of alternatives be independent of information concerning alternatives not in that set.[9]

It might be thought that such a prohibition is unnecessary, since normally a device will not even have such extraneous information available to it. In an election among Nixon, Carter, and Wallace, a device just is not going to "find out" how voters feel about Willy Brandt. But this takes too narrow a view. As Arrow points out, there is always the possibility of a person's candidacy being terminated after the voting has occurred but before the results have been officially certified. With respect to the surviving candidates, the eliminated one is an irrelevant (extraneous, unfeasible) alternative. Yet, by hypothesis, the device does have information about voters' preferences toward him. (In de-

9. Independent of what kind of information? Since we have already discussed the issue of ordinality, we shall not re-raise that question here. Let it be understood that the information adverted to is whatever kind is finally decided upon as relevant and appropriate to social choice, be that ordinal, cardinal, or what have you. The independence aspect of (I) is itself independent of its ordinality aspect, and can be grafted onto any satisfactory resolution of that issue. If only bare order of preference is deemed appropriate, then independence requires that the social outcome be independent of information concerning preference *orderings* of alternatives not in the alternative set. If intensity information is thought appropriate, then independence requires the social ranking to be independent of information concerning the individuals' preference *intensities* toward alternatives not in. And so on.

cathlon scoring, a contestant might be disqualified after the events have all been run and the results reported.) In fact each subset of a given set of alternatives can be viewed as "reachable" by possible choice-alternative eliminations. Thus, as noted in chapter 2, in a certain sense the independence aspect of requirement (I) ensures that the social ordering is built up out of (or decomposible into) successive pairwise comparisons. In short, independence requires that the way members of any subgroup get ranked in the social ranking of the whole group be independent of information concerning alternatives not in that subgroup. A pair being a subgroup, the relative positions of any pair in the social ranking of any number of alternatives must depend only on information concerning that pair.

So that is what independence requires. Now why should it be thought reasonable to require that? One motivation is to rule out any back-door, indirect attempts at extracting preference intensities from preference orderings. Such attempts try to infer intensity "distances" by comparing the way a given pair of alternatives situate in the ordering with respect to some (irrelevant) third(s). But beyond reinforcing ordinality, is there anything else to be said for independence?

There appear to be two main points at which information about "irrelevant" alternatives might influence social choice. It might condition the formation of individuals' preferences toward the "relevant" alternatives, so that the raw material, so to speak, supplied to a device would incorporate certain "irrelevant" influences from the outset. Or, the influence might enter only at the aggregation stage, the raw material remaining untainted. We mention the former possiblity only to set it aside. Requirement (I) has nothing to do with the *formation* of individuals' preferences. It is concerned entirely with how a device processes the information it gets (however that might have been formed). So, it is in the aggregation process, not in the formation of individual preferences, that (I) bars any "irrelevant" influence. But why, exactly, should it do this? We shall let Arrow speak for himself, at some length, on this.

Suppose that an election system has been devised whereby each individual lists all the candidates in order of his preference and then, by a preassigned procedure, the winning candidate is derived from these lists. . . . Suppose that an election is held, with a certain number of candidates in the field, each individual filing his list of preferences, and then one of the candidates dies. Surely the social choice should be made by taking each of the individual's preference lists, blotting out completely the dead candidate's name, and considering only the orderings of the remaining names in going through the procedure of determining the winner. That is, the choice to be made among the set of surviving candidates should be independent of the preferences of individuals for candidates not in S. To assume otherwise would be to make the result of the election dependent on the obviously accidental circumstance of whether a candidate died before or after the date of polling. Therefore, we may require of our social welfare function that the choice made by society from a given environment depend only on the orderings of individuals among the alternatives in that environment. Alternatively stated, if we consider two sets of individual orderings such that, for each individual, his ordering of those particular alternatives in a given environment is the same each time, then we require that the choice made by society from that environment be the same when the individual values are given by the first set of orderings as they are when given by the second.

. . . The reasonableness of this condition can be seen by consideration of the possible results in a method of choice which does not satisfy [it], the rank-order method of voting frequently used in clubs. With a finite number of candidates, let each individual rank all the candidates, i.e., designate his first-choice candidate, second-choice candidate, etc. Let preassigned weights be given to the first, second, etc., choices, the higher weight to the higher choice, and then let the candidate with the highest weighted sum of votes be elected. In particular, suppose that there are three voters and four candidates, x, y, z, and w. Let the weights for the first, second, third, and fourth choices be 4, 3, 2, and 1, respectively. Suppose that individuals 1 and 2 rank the candidates in the order x, y, z, and w, while individual 3 ranks them in the order z, w, x, and y. Under the given electoral system, x is chosen. Then, certainly, if y is deleted from the ranks of the candidates, the system applied to the remaining candidates should yield the same result, especially since, in this case, y is inferior to x according to the tastes of every individual; but, if y is in fact deleted, the indicated electoral system would yield a tie between x and z.[10]

We will examine these two cases—the dead candidate, and rank-order voting—separately, in the order presented. Concerning the dead candidate, some might think such an awkwardly timed death would justify holding a new election. With that candidate not available, some voters might revise their preferences for the survivors if they had the chance. But (I), as we remarked, is not concerned with the *formation* of individual preferences. So we may neutralize this distraction by assuming that even if a new election were held, the voters' relative preferences for the surviving candidates would not differ at all from what they were in the original polling. So holding a new election under this neutralizing hypothesis would be tantamount to doing what Arrow claims is the reasonable thing, namely, "taking each of the individual's preference lists, blotting out completely the dead candidate's name, and considering only the orderings of the remaining names in going through the procedure of determining the winner."

The point then, is not that the death of a candidate should not make any difference to the social choice among the survivors.

10. Kenneth J. Arrow, *Social Choice and Individual Values*, 2d. ed., pp. 26–27.

The point is that it should not make a difference *if* no individual's preference ordering (of any survivor) is changed. In short, if the input (the individual orderings) from the diminished candidate set is exactly what it was before, then the output (social ordering) from the diminished set should be exactly what *it* was before, that is, when it was embedded in the larger set. Why? Because otherwise we should have the output depending on (or, being responsive to) factors other than those intended. As Arrow puts it, the outcome of the election would depend on "the obviously accidental circumstance of whether a candidate died before or after the date of polling." It is intended that the social choice between two alternatives, x and y, depends on certain sorts of previously agreed relevant information; whether ordinal, cardinal, or what have you. But whatever that might be, it presumably does not include the circumstance that some third alternative, z, died before or after, say, November 4, 1984.

The general point, then, is that we do not want social choice to be at the hazard of unintended factors. If we did want it to depend on candidate longevity or date of demise—for whatever reason: perhaps the date on which a qualified candidate dies is a matter of astrological or religious significance and hence thought to deserve an impact on social choice—then provision for that should be deliberately built in and explicitly acknowledged.

The second case, rank-order voting, provides a more elaborate illustration of the possibilities for mischief that need guarding against. The point is not just that we do not want unintended factors having an influence on social choice. Part of the point is that some such influences have a tendency to slip in unnoticed. Hence, we need to take measures to exclude them, like requiring independence. We do not, after all, frame requirements to bar all possible ways in which a device might go wrong. Only the most salient, those which present a clear and present danger, call for explicit counter-measures.[11]

Rank-order voting can be thought of as a very crude, back-door, indirect attempt at responding to preference intensities. The numbers (preassigned weightings) associated with the positions or ranks in the individuals' preference scales—that is, last choice gets assigned one point, next last gets two, third from last, three, and so forth—these numbers can be thought of as representing crude approximations to intensity measures. Of course, the imposition of any particular set of numbers as opposed to any other set which is compatible with the gross ordinal rankings is somewhat arbitrary; and similarly for imposing the same range of numbers for different individuals. As far as the underlying psychological realities go, imposing any particular set of order-preserving numbers (and imposing them uniformly across people) is as likely as not to falsify actual preference-intensity relations. Not all cardinalizations, nor even all attempts to squeeze cardinal blood out of an ordinal turnip, are as clumsy as this; but rank-order voting is. Anyhow, after imposing these numbers the device proceeds to perform operations upon them (summing them) and it generates its final output based on the results of these operations.

What violates the independence requirement is this. When,

11. Independence plays somewhat the role for aggregation devices that considerations of rigor play for a logical system. Illicit, unacknowledged premises sneaking in, subtle fallacies committed in complex reasonings, these are sources of logical sin by which we are constantly beset. The precepts of rigor are designed to bar *them*, but not to remedy all possible ways of going wrong. Typing errors, excessive haste, inattention, and many other factors can spoil a proof. But they are not the sort of thing rigor is designed to preclude. Likewise, other things can go wrong with an aggregation device than just its responding to factors not intended. But we do not construct separate requirements to rule all of them out.

to go back to Arrow's example, alternative y is deleted—all else in the way of individual preference orderings remaining the same—the device reassigns (a different set of) numbers to the surviving alternatives, at least as arbitrarily as before. However, when it then performs its operation (summing) on the new numbers and bases its new social ranking on them, the social ordering of some of the survivors is different from what it was in the original.

We can provisionally distinguish at least two features of this device which might be considered objectionable: (1) it can be interpreted as an attempt to respond, however crudely, to preference intensities, and (2) it is somewhat arbitrary. The former matter we shall not go into here. It merely re-raises the substantive question of ordinality versus cardinality, an issue on which we have already passed. The arbitrariness, however, of the rank-order method is quite independent of its sensitivity to intensities per se, as can be easily shown. Consider a device, call it D, which *is* sensitive to preference intensities. It performs operations (summing) on numbers which reflect individual preference intensities, and bases its social rankings on the results of these operations. But, unlike rank-order voting, it does not *itself* impose the numbers it operates upon. Instead, they are supplied it by some independent means which, by hypothesis, accurately reflects the individuals' underlying psychological realities. In short, D is just like rank-order voting in what it does with the numbers after it gets them. But D is supplied the numbers it uses as part of its original information, the input data that it gets. Rank-order voting, on the other hand, is originally supplied only ordinal information (individuals' preference orderings) as its input data. It itself imposes the numbers it then proceeds to respond to. In the gap between the supplied preference orderings and the device-imposed numbers there lies considerable scope for arbitrariness. But this does not yet capture the crucial feature. So far it looks like all the objection amounts to is merely that, as far as accuracy of correlation between actual preference intensities and their (imposed) numerical representations goes, the imposed numbers have no better than a random chance of getting it right. But things are even worse than that. Not only would it be dumb luck if the original number assignments reflected actual preference intensity distances, but the device has a built-in, systematic bias which makes its number imposition scheme worse than random in this regard.

The rank-order method somewhat arbitrarily imposes its own numbers; but, as Arrow's example also demonstrates, in certain circumstances it can require the imposition of different numbers —for example, upon deletion of an alternative, all else remaining the same—again without any real relation to the underlying psychological realities. That is, not only had the original numerical imposition no very firm basis in the underlying psychological realities, but the (automatically forced) changed numeration testifies to a change in intensities that need not really have taken place. This is not just more arbitrariness, but is especially objectionable.

It is in fact possible for a device that is sensitive to preference intensities to violate requirement (I) honestly, as it were. Because it is possible for individual's preference intensities to change (within limits) without their preference orderings changing. A person might rank four candidates in the order x, y, z, w, with intensities $x = 4$, $y = 3$, $z = 2$, and $w = 1$; and after y is deleted, still place the survivors in the same preference *order* as before (namely, x, z, w), but change the intensities of his preferences (within the boundaries allowed by the unchanged order) to, say, $x = 3$, $z = 2$, and $w = 1$. Although still preferred to z and w, x's intensity distance from them is considerably diminished from what it was before y's deletion. As far as abstract possibilities go, such a deletion might, for a given individual, leave both order and intensity of preferences toward the survivors unchanged. Or it might result in a change of intensity distances, but not preference order. Or it might change both. The a priori possibilities are all open as far as the underlying psychological realities are concerned. Now requirement (I) can only be violated, in any case, if all individual preference *orderings* remain unchanged (upon deletion of some alternative). That is the circumstance which triggers (I)'s applicability. If preference orderings change, then no matter what the device does it cannot violate (I). But it is one thing for a device to violate (I) if (because) intensities *do* change in such "triggering" circumstances. It is quite another thing for the device itself to create such a change (*ex nihilo*, in a manner of speaking) and then, responding to the very change it has created, to violate (I). The former might be reasonable, depending what we think about the substance of the ordinality/cardinality issue. The latter is plainly unreasonable no matter what.

Consider the alternatives x and z (in Arrow's example) before the deletion of y, and then after. As regards underlying psychological realities, such a deletion might or might not result in a change in intensity of preference regarding x and z on the part of any individual. The rank-order method, both systematically (in one sense) and arbitrarily (in another), demands that it does result in such an intensity change for individuals 1 and 2, but not for individual 3. That is, the device itself requires that deleting y *reduce* the intensity of preference which individuals 1 and 2 have for x over z, while not effecting any change in the intensity of preference which individual 3 has for z over x. Thus, it is no wonder that z's position in the overall ranking is enhanced at x's expense.

But what is objectionable about this is not that the device reranked x and z in the diminished setting (from x defeating z to z and x tying). What offends is that it did so on a perfectly arbitrary basis, one that bore no relation to the actual underlying psychological realities such a device is intended to respond to. After all, if you have a device like D which is designed to be sensitive to preference intensities, you would want it to respond to changes in intensities *if they occur*. What is peculiarly objectionable about rank-order voting is not that it infringes ordinality by responding to changes in preference intensities. If that is an offense, then *D* is guilty of that. Rank-order voting is much worse: it arbitrarily manufactures the very intensity changes that it then proceeds to respond to.

The general moral is that we do not want a device to be creative, to have a life of its own. We want it to be responsive to certain kinds of data (ordinal, cardinal, or whatever) which we have independently decided are appropriate to social choice. But we do not want the device arbitrarily creating the data to which it then responds. Logicians who treat of the theory of definitions have a requirement, called *noncreativity*, which is closely related to what we have been discussing. They hold that definitions whose sole intended function is abbreviation— notational economy—should be noncreative in the sense that one should not be able to generate new theorems, after introducing the definition, which were not derivable before. The idea is that the definition—being merely a notational, shorthand convenience—should not have a life of its own, making substantive, unintended contributions (that is, new theorems) to the system. It is a notion very much like that that the independence aspect requirement (I) is intended to enforce. In words, not worrying overmuch about mathematical tractability, we might describe the rationale behind (I) as follows:

(1) Whatever sorts of data we think it desirable that a device be responsive to, we want the device to be sensitive just to that and nothing else. In particular, we do not want a device to be creative, to have a life of its own, arbitrarily

87

creating and then responding to its own data. It should just do what it is told.

(2) The only sort of information that a device should respond to is individuals' order of preference.

Our analysis of (I) then follows the general strategy of our earlier approach to the obtainability issue separating ordinalists and cardinalists. There, it will be remembered, we viewed the particular injunction, Do not use intensity information!, as deriving from the general injunction, Do not use any information that canr ɔt be reliably obtained!, and the particular claim, Intensity informa ion cannot be reliably had. So here, we analyze (I) into two parts; a general directive of noncreativity: A device should respond only to the information intended; and a commitment setting the bounds of what is to count as creativity: only information concerning preference orderings is intended. The actual details of the formulation of (I)—its pairwise-choice format—derive their support from the fact that they turn out to be a way of accomplishing those general aims, namely, guaranteeing noncreativity on an ordinal base. As before, this analytical strategy enables us to factor out various things that would otherwise be run together, a virtue that will become apparent later.

This concludes our detailed examination of the elements which jointly lead to Arrow's Impossibility Theorem. We have gone about as far as it will be useful to go down this route of separately analyzing and assessing for independent plausibility each of the four, conflict-generating requirements—five, if we include the background assumption of logical well-behavedness. The pieces of the puzzle are now out on the table: unlimited scope, the Pareto principle, nondictatorship, and independence of irrelevant alternatives. What remains is to fit them together to achieve some sort of explanatory gestalt.

5

Some Ways Out

Assuming the proof of Arrow's impossibility result valid, which of the four conditions on rationality should we give up? An answer to this will not necessarily provide the kind of explanation-cum-understanding we are seeking, but it might point the way to one. (In a well-designed conceptual universe, an explanation that resolved the puzzlingness of a paradox would focus on the most dispensable premise that generated it. As rationalists, we may hope.) Without attempting anything like comprehensiveness, a survey of some of the main options for avoiding Arrow's result might be useful. According to our analysis in chapter 2, the Pareto principle and nondictatorship are relatively untouchable. But unlimited scope and independence of irrelevant alternatives are fair game, as is the standing background assumption of logical well-behavedness. We will consider them in reverse order.

As regards logical well-behavedness, an obvious way out of Arrow's paradox is to give up transitivity. Since we treated this issue at some length in chapter 3, we can be briefer here. It is often assumed that there is a single, unitary concept of preference instanced by both individual and society, which has a single, unitary set of logical features. There are not, then, separate questions about social preference and individual preference; there are just questions about preference. So, to decide whether social preference is transitive, it suffices to determine whether individual preference is transitive. At least the latter bears importantly on the former. This was the approach we took in chapter 3, where we argued (negatively) for transitivity.

Another approach assumes that there are distinct issues here: that to speak of "social preference" is to use terminology nonliterally, there being no psychological structure, no unified mind of a "social individual," to support it. Hence, the decision as to what logical features social preference has is, if not totally unconstrained by, at least substantially independent of, the truth about individual preference. In particular, individual preference might be transitive and social preference not. (In which case it would seem best not to use the same word for the two relations.) Viewed in this way, cups-of-coffee counterexamples, and strategies to defuse them, are alike beside the point. What, then, does count?

Even if social and individual preference are distinct, they share one feature which provides perhaps the strongest argument for transitivity (our intuitions about individual preference aside); that is, they share connections between preference, choice, and behavior. Nontransitive, circular, or cyclical preferences, whether individual or social, do not provide determinate, satisfactory, unambiguous directives for action. If we are charged with executing social policy on the basis of social preference, and we discover that society prefers A to B to C to A, then we are without definite guidance. For any alternative chosen, there is another socially preferred to it.

To this it might be objected that in the case of cyclical preferences, the appropriate action would be either (a) do nothing, or (b) treat all alternatives in the cycle as socially indifferent. Against (a), it is possible that "do nothing" (that is, retain the status quo) is itself one of the items in the preference cycle,[1] in

1. This point was well made by the Rev. C. L. Dodgson (Lewis Carroll). See Duncan Black's historical discussion in *The Theory of Committees and Elections*, p. 220.

which case there is some alternative socially preferred to it. As against (b), a preference cycle is not in fact a case of social indifference: xIy, yIz, and zIx imply not xPy, not yPz, and not zPx, each of which is contradicted by the preference cycle xPy, yPz, zPx. If it is replied that, although not strictly a case of social indifference, it should be treated as if it were one; one response might be to demand a reason for so doing—a reason independent[2] of the (ad hoc) desire to escape from a sticky difficulty. Further, not every social-choice mechanism even has a way of treating social indifference. Some, like majority rule with a tie-breaking mechanism, contain provisions that prevent it from occurring. For these, the injunction to treat preference cycles as if they were instances of social indifference is empty. It does not succeed in specifying a way to treat them.

Turning next to the independence of irrelevant alternatives, Arrow has suggested it as the most eligible for modification (or elimination).[3] Some would take the simple route of infringing the ordinality aspect of (I) directly, and allowing appeal to preference intensity. Failing satisfactory resolution of the problem of interpersonal comparisons, this way out seems problematic. Arrow has further suggested[4] that the concept of extended sympathy might be of assistance here. The idea is this. Suppose that I want to compare my intensity of preference for y over x with your intensity of preference for x over y. I do it by asking myself whether I would prefer to be myself in the situation where y obtains, or to be you in the situation where x does. This implies that I can judge how intensely you prefer x to y by imaginatively projecting myself into your shoes and asking (myself as thus trans-

2. That is, we want to see a reason which is persuasive when the facts about preference cycles are considered on their own merits, independent of the fact that, together with other things, they generate difficulties.
3. Arrow, "Values and Collective Decision Making," p. 232.
4. Ibid.

91

posed) how strongly "I" prefer x to y. (It assumes that each person can reliably detect preference intensity in himself.) Its attractions are twofold: (1) it replaces an intensity question with a question of bare preference—you are finally asked only to choose between two (complex) options: being yourself in one situation, and being him in another—and (2) whatever comparisons are implicitly made, everything goes on in one skull, neatly bypassing the impenetrability of other minds.

This way out does not seem all that attractive either. It is rather like comparing results from the hurdles and the shot put by asking how far 0.21 second would be if time were distance. The notorious difficulties of interpretation encountered by philosophers and modal logicians in dealing with subjunctive, counterfactual, cross-possible-world identifications—what A would be if it were B—give a sober person pause.

But there are other branches of this same family of ways out, since there are other features of condition (I) than its ordinality aspect. As our analysis in chapters 2 and 4 showed, there is also the requirement of noncreativity, and the pairwise-choice format. Noncreativity seems a good thing, but what about pairwise choice? This requires that the social ranking of every pair of alternatives be whatever it is regardless of anything about the rest of the setting it happens to be embedded in. This aspect of condition (I) derives its support from the fact that it turns out to be a way of guaranteeing noncreativity on an ordinal base. It is important to distinguish noncreativity itself, which we admit to be a reasonable requirement, from the means used to achieve it, namely, pairwise choice. Composing a group choice out of successive pairwise comparisons does not appear to have much intrinsically to recommend it. Its main visible means of support derives from the fact that it is a mathematically tractable way of enforcing noncreativity. If it should cease to do that, or if, in doing so it has other undesirable side effects—and there are other ways to ensure noncreativity which lack them—then we could dispense with pairwise choice without much regret. And even if we could not find a ready substitute, some (equally) mathematically tractable requirement which would do the job pairwise choice does, but without its (so far merely hinted at) undesirable side effects, we could still give it up if we had to. After all, it is merely a gimmick to prevent us from making a certain sort of tempting, easy to make but hard to detect, mistake. Like the precepts of rigor—listing all primitive notions, axioms, formation and transformation rules; writing everything out explicitly; and so forth—if you meet the requirements it is guaranteed that you will not make that sort of mistake, but if you do not meet them it does not follow that you will. This, then, is a possibility worth exploring: to evade Arrow's result, keep (U), (P), (D), and both the ordinality and noncreativity aspects of (I), but give up its pairwise-choice format.

Pairwise choice (PWC) means that in socially ranking any pair of candidates a device cannot respond to information about other candidates, nor to any other information not about the pair in question. This prohibition, laudable in many respects, has one unobvious implication that is troubling. It constrains not only the content of information a device can respond to, it also restricts the (logical) form such information can come in. In particular, it does not permit a device to respond to a certain kind of general information, which we shall call *global information*, about settings considered as totalities. Here is what that means. Consider the following social-choice rule:

(R1)   For any two alternatives *X* and *Y* in a setting, a device will socially rank *X* above *Y* if and only if *X* is preferred to *Y* *and to every other alternative* in the setting by at least a majority of the individuals in the setting.

Let us say that alternative *X* has a *majority coalition* against alternative *Y* when at least a majority of voters prefers *X* to *Y*. A *majority alternative* will be one that has majority coalitions against all other alternatives in a setting. (R1) says that an alternative can be socially ranked above another if and only if it is a majority alternative.

On the face of it, (R1) is as ordinalistic as one might want. All it speaks of is bare preference; no hidden appeals to intensity information or anything like that. Still, it is incompatible with PWC, because implementing it requires global information. Whether a setting contains a majority alternative, and hence, whether a given alternative is majority alternative in a setting, is a global fact about that setting. It depends on how all the alternatives fare vis-à-vis each other in the voters' preference orderings, not on the preference standings of any less-than-total subgroup, and in particular, not just on the relative orderings of any pair. A majority alternative commands majority coalitions against *all* the other alternatives. What is it about whether a majority alternative is present that escapes determination by pairwise comparison? Quite simply, it is the fact that one has checked them all. It can be determined—solely on the basis of pairwise comparisons—about each alternative and each other alternative that one either is or is not preferred to the other by a majority of voters in a setting. But while in doing this all pairs may in fact have been checked, the fact that they have cannot itself be determined by pairwise comparisons. To determine that a given alternative is majority alternative in a setting you have to know not only about him and (what are in fact) each of the others, that he is preferred to it by a majority, you must also know *that you know that about them all.*

Let us use the term *global constraint* for a rule that constrains what a device does when an alternative bears some stated relation to all the other alternatives in a setting. (R1), then, is a global constraint. Responding to global constraints conflicts with the PWC format of independence of irrelevant alternatives, because whether or not a global constraint is activated depends on how the totality of alternatives in a setting relate to each other. So to know whether a setting contains a majority alternative, say—and hence, whether the global constraint (R1) is triggered—it is not enough to know of each pair of alternatives how they stand in all the voters' preferences. You also need to know that you know that for all of them. The former is PWC-available, but the latter is not. The reason why it is not involves a simple logical point.

The generality expressed by an "all" statement is not decomposible without remainder into the sum of its particular, nongeneral parts (or instances). Thus, the universal generalization, "All inventors of the calculus were geniuses," is not equivalent to the nongeneral conjunction of particular statements, "N. invented the calculus and was a genius," and "So did and was L."—even though it is true, as a matter of fact, that N. and L. exhaust the set of calculus inventors. To close the gap one must add the statement, "N. and L. were all the inventors of the calculus there were," which, of course, provides closure only at the cost of reintroducing another "all" claim. In short, one cannot establish that

All A's are B's.

by finding out that

a is a B, b is a B, c is a B, . . ., n is a B.

no matter how many of these particular claims are separately verified, not even if all things that are in fact A's get checked and turn out to be B's. Because no amount of such particular claims will ever imply a universal generalization. To get the implication one needs to add to the particular claims the closure statement,

And that is all the A's there are.

95

which itself expresses universal generality.[5] Hence, the statement

X is majority alternative in setting S.

which implicitly involves the global generality built into the concept of a majority alternative, is not implied by a conjunction of particular claims, such as:

X is preferred to Y by a majority of voters in S, and
X is preferred to Z by a majority of voters in S, and
X is preferred to W by a majority of voters in S

even if $X, Y, Z,$ and W in fact exhaust the alternatives in setting S. To get the desired implication, one needs the closure statement,

5. Russell, in "The Philosophy of Logical Atomism," puts the point this way.

You cannot ever arrive at a general fact by inference from particular facts, however numerous. The old plan of complete induction, which used to occur in books, which was always supposed to be quite safe and easy as opposed to ordinary induction, that plan of complete induction, unless it is accompanied by at least one general proposition, will not yield you the result you want. Suppose, for example, that you wish to prove in that way that 'All men are mortal', you are supposed to proceed by complete induction, and say 'A is a man that is mortal', 'B is a man that is mortal', 'C is a man that is mortal', and so on until you finish. You will not be able, in that way, to arrive at the proposition 'All men are mortal' unless you know when you have finished. That is to say that, in order to arrive by this road at the general proposition 'All men are mortal', you must already have the general proposition 'All men are among those I have enumerated'. You never can arrive at a general proposition by inference from particular propositions alone. You will always have to have at least one general proposition in your premises. [From Bertrand Russell, *Logic and Knowledge*, ed. Robert C. Marsh (New York: G. P. Putnam's Sons, 1971), p. 235].

All the alternatives in setting S are among those I have enumerated.

which again contains global generality. Now pairwise choice is a filter through which this kind of generality—universal generalizations, about all alternatives in a setting—cannot pass. It permits particular statements about alternatives—for instance, that one bears a certain relation to another—but screens out every last vestige of the magic word "all." This is because, as will be recalled, in the social ranking of a pair of alternatives it only allows a device to respond to information about that pair. But the news that some alternative is a majority alternative in a setting, or, more generally, the information that a setting contains a majority alternative, cannot be inferred from any amount of data derived exclusively from facts about pairs of alternatives. No fact about all alternatives in a setting can be derived from facts about pairs of alternatives, even if the setting contains only two alternatives. Generality never results from the mere conjunction of particulars.

In previous discussion we have remarked that condition (I) imposes a restriction on the substance or content of information available to an aggregation device: it restricts it to information about preference orderings. Now it emerges that it, or anyhow its pairwise-choice format, places an equally severe restriction on the form in which otherwise acceptable information can come. Only particular, never (universally) general information about alternatives can be available to a device that satisfies (I), no matter what its content—ordinal, cardinal, or what have you.

Now, on the face of it, this fact about the PWC format of condition (I)—that it excludes all global information no matter what its content—is the sort of consideration we have been seeking: independent reason, just from considering the thing on its merits, not from its complicity in the Arrow paradox, for doubting that it is a reasonable thing to require of any aggregation device, a canon of rationality for social choice. There does not appear to be anything intrinsically suspect about global information merely on account of its generality. Yet it is on this ground alone that pairwise choice rules it out.

Such is the attractiveness, if it can be done, of retaining Arrow's conditions (U), unlimited scope, (P), the Pareto principle, (D), nondictatorship, and both the ordinality and the noncreativity aspects of (I), independence of irrelevant alternatives, but giving up the latter's pairwise-choice format. But is this feasible? Can we really give up pairwise choice and still retain both the noncreativity and the ordinality aspects of condition (I)?

When it comes to the issue of preference orderings versus preference intensities, we can continue to plump for preference orderings. But other information will have to be recognized as (possibly) appropriate and relevant to social choice. What other information? Well, none that is in the same line of work as information about individuals' preference orderings, so to speak. Not, for example, preference intensities or anything that might be thought of as a natural competitor of preference orderings. (Not, for instance, health, wealth, race, color, creed, or anything like that.) But we will have to admit the (possible) relevance of global information about the preference ordering contour or shape of settings as a whole, totalities. Their ingredients, as it were, can still be restricted to information about individuals' preference orderings. But global information about the totality of preferences will not itself be just another ingredient.

The intuitive point behind an ordinality requirement is, *operating at the level of ingredients*, to admit preference-ordering information and exclude its natural competitors. But pursuant to that, the social ranking of any pair of alternatives in any setting need not strictly depend only on information concerning individuals' preference orderings of that pair. Not because it should depend on information about preference intensities, or anything else (deemed inappropriate) at the ingredients level. Because it can legitimately depend in part on global information about whole settings, totalities of preference orderings, such as whether there exists a majority alternative in a given setting. Consider what we might call Quaker voting procedures. They set a premium on unanimity, with its (implicit) noncoerciveness. One such procedure—the unanimity counterpart of (R1) —is this.

(Q1) An alternative shall be socially ranked above another if and only if it is unanimously preferred to all others in the setting.

One might think such a rule ill-advised for any number of reasons. It may foster social conservatism through favoring the status quo. It may increase intragroup animosities. It may leave social conflict unresolved overlong. It gives each voter absolute veto over group decisions. It may be unworkable for a reasonably large and diverse population. But does it violate ordinality? Nobody's preference intensities are consulted. (It may be that only persons with intense preferences will be willing to brave group displeasure by exercising their veto, but it also may not. Perhaps rugged individualists will do it often, frivolously.) Concerning any individual's preferences, only their order counts. To work the thing, in addition to knowing who prefers what to what, all you have to do is count votes. And although the device does respond to global information—facts about how one alternative relates to all the rest—its ingredients are purely ordinal individual preferences.

We are considering giving up pairwise choice, and hence condition (I) in Arrow's formulation. But we want to retain some commitment to ordinality and we certainly do not want to violate noncreativity, whether it is an explicitly stated requirement or not. The former is readily managed. We just say what we mean. Call it condition (O).

(O) (Ordinality): A device shall not respond to any information *concerning the preferences of any individual toward any alternatives* except information about the order of that individual's preferences.

The idea is to restrict the operation of the requirement to what we called the level of ingredients: when it comes to information about any particular individual, all we want to know from him is the order of his preferences toward the alternatives. But that does not rule out global information, because that is not information about any particular individual.

It is probably best to leave our commitment to noncreativity unstated. Now that global information is recognized as relevant, there is no longer an obvious, simple, mathematically tractable way to express a noncreativity requirement. Generalized injunctions to noncreativity are a bit gratuitous anyway. In general terms, noncreativity is just a particular application of the injunction to be intelligent, to do what you intend and not something else. It is hardly feasible, after all, to incorporate specific prohibitions against each possible path of error. So allowing unintended side effects to creep in unnoticed—the particular hazard that noncreativity defends against—probably does not deserve honorable mention.

We might try then giving up PWC yet keeping Arrow's requirements (U), (P), and (D), by replacing his (I) with our (O), plus observing a no longer explicitly stated commitment to noncreativity. The latter two elements—condition (O), together with (implicit) noncreativity—capture what was originally attractive about Arrow's requirement (I), without burdening us with its pairwise-choice format. If we take this way out, however, we should be clear what it involves. Pairwise choice is gone: what used to count as violations of (I) in that regard can now freely occur unchastized. In particular, it will no longer be prohibited for some pair of alternatives to be socially ranked one way in one setting and a different way in another, even though all individual preference orderings remain constant. Everything will depend on the character of the extra factor(s) (if any) involved. The reason for the difference in social ranking will have to be sought out and examined. The difference per se will no longer be decisive. If the additional factor is relevant and appropriate to social choice, then what previously would have constituted a violation of (I) will be blameless. If not, then our (now implicit) noncreativity requirement condemns it, although not mechanically as it used to.

This is, of course, only the barest sketch of one possible way out of Arrow's paradox. Its ramifications certainly need more extensive development and investigation than we have given them here. In particular, the following points should be noted.

(1) Although we have strongly suggested that it is so, we have not strictly established either that or how Arrow's four conditions on rationality jointly require that a device respond to global information. So even if the filtering out of such information does count against pairwise choice, does constitute independent reason for giving it up, and even if giving up pairwise choice would avoid Arrow's result, still we should only have escaped from, not resolved the puzzlingness of, Arrow's paradox. (It will not have been ruled out, for example, that there is some other fact about pairwise choice which is the "real" culprit.)

(2) Although we have strongly suggested that it is so, we have not strictly shown that the proposed remedy, giving up pairwise choice, really would be effective. And, perhaps most important,

(3) even if that remedy was effective against Arrow's paradox, it does not look like it would dent the paradox of voting, or related phenomena. Yet the puzzlingness of these closely resembles that of Arrow's paradox, which is, in some sense, a generalization of them. Ideally, we would like an explanation that would handle all these matters uniformly, not resolve and explain Arrow's paradox but leave these other, similar paradoxes untouched.

101

Some Ways Out

Which brings us to that family of ways out that work by violating condition (U), unlimited scope. As we noted in chapter 2, there are various restrictions that might be imposed concerning what preference patterns a device should or should not accept. For instance, there is a single-peakedness, the requirement that from among every triple of alternatives in an acceptable preference pattern there be one which all voters agree is not worst. Such restrictions avoid Arrow's result by ruling out of court the paradox of voting and related problematic phenomena. In earlier discussion we dismissed such moves as ad hoc and unmotivated, except for the (unworthy) desire to avoid paradox. While conceding that unlimited scope was not a conceptual necessity for rational social choice, we nevertheless maintained that it was a defeasible requirement of desirability (that is, *ceteris paribus* a good thing), and thus independent reason was needed for infringing it.

In our final chapter we will suggest a way of thinking about both Arrow's paradox and the paradox of voting which provides one sort of independent motivation for infringing unlimited scope and accepting a single-peakedness-type pattern restriction on social choice. We shall there urge that both Arrow's paradox and the paradox of voting involve versions of an infinite regress argument, and that accepting a single-peakedness restriction amounts to the traditional escape from a regress: positing a first cause.

In preparation for that we shall, in the next chapter, prove a version of Arrow's Theorem chosen to expose the role of condition (U), unlimited scope. It is, anyhow, time we had a look at an actual proof of this famous result.

6

Arrow's Theorem

I. The Premises

Arrow's Theorem is an impossibility result about aggregation devices: procedures (or rules, or functions) for combining individual preferences to obtain a collective choice. The theorem shows that, given a certain standing background assumption, no aggregation device can jointly satisfy the following "rationality" conditions:

Condition 1. Unrestricted scope (U). A device should accept as input any logically coherent set of individual preferences for any finite group of choice alternatives.

Condition 2. Pareto principle (P). Unanimity should be implemented. If x is preferred to y by all individuals without exception, then x should be socially preferred to y.

Condition 3. Nondictatorship (D). No single voter's preferences should automatically be made the social preference regardless of the preferences of all other voters.

Condition 4. Independence of irrelevant alternatives (I). The social ordering of any given set of alternatives should depend only on the individuals' preference orderings of those alternatives.

Standing background assumption: Preference and indifference, both individual and social, should be logically well-behaved. That is,

(i) they should be *transitive*: if x is preferred to y, and y is preferred to z, then x is preferred to z, and likewise for indifference, and

(ii) they should be *connected*: for any two alternatives x and y, either x is preferred to y, or y is preferred to x, or x and y are indifferent.

In Arrow's original proof (*Social Choice and Individual Values*, 1951) there were five conditions. Instead of condition 2 above, it had

Condition 2a. Positive association of social and individual values (PA). If x is socially preferred to y, any changes in individual preferences that do not worsen x's position relative to y in any individual's preference should not worsen x's social ranking relative to y; and

Condition 2b. Citizens' sovereignty (CS). There is no social preference that cannot be generated by some set of individual preferences; that is, no social preference is taboo.

These two conditions imply the Pareto principle,[1] so Arrow's

---

1. Because take any setting where x is socially preferred to y. Either it contains unanimity for x over y or it does not. If it does, then when all individuals prefer x to y, society does too. If it does not, then there are some individuals who do not prefer x to y. Now changing all their preferences to achieve unanimity for x over y involves nothing but changes in x's favor relative to y, so by condition 2a, x must continue

later, more compact proof (*Social Choice and Individual Values*, 1963) that the four conditions are inconsistent also constitutes a proof that the original five are.

II. The Proof

We define the following special notions:

D.1 A *setting* is a group of voters and candidates, together with the voters' preferences toward the candidates.

D.2 A setting that contains every voter is *maximal*.

D.3 A device is *vicious* if there is a maximal setting where one voter prefers x to y, all other voters prefer y to x, and the device ranks x above y.

D.4 A device is *dictatorial* if there is an individual K such that for every pair of candidates x and y, the device ranks x above y in every setting where K prefers x to y.

Our proof uses conditions (U), (P), (PA), (I), and (D), thus falling intermediate (in terms of logical strength) between Arrow's earlier, five-condition, and his later, four-condition proofs. It is designed to expose the role of condition (U), and, incidentally, to clear up certain quantifier ambiguities that have been thought to darken other proofs. We proceed in two stages: (1) first showing that any device that satisfies unlimited scope and the Pareto principle must be vicious; then (2) that a vicious device which satisfies all the other conditions must be dictatorial. From this it follows that no device can jointly satisfy conditions (U), (P), (PA), (I), and (D).

Lemma 1. Any device that satisfies (U) and (P) must be vicious.

---

socially preferred to y. So if any setting yields x socially preferred to y, unanimity will. And by condition 2b, some setting does yield x socially preferred to y. Therefore, conditions 2a and 2b imply condition 2, the Pareto principle: if all individuals prefer x to y, society does, too.

105

Arrow's Theorem

Proof. By unlimited scope, maximal setting S is admissible.

$$S = \begin{array}{c} v_1: \\ v_2: \\ v_3: \\ \vdots \\ v_m \end{array} \begin{bmatrix} c_1 & c_2 & \cdots & \cdots & c_m \\ c_m & c_1 & c_2 & \cdots & c_{m-1} \\ c_{m-1} & c_m & c_1 & c_2 & \cdots \\ & & & & \vdots \\ c_2 & \cdots & c_{m-1} & c_m & c_1 \end{bmatrix}$$

(We represent a setting by an $m \times n$ matrix where the m individuals head the rows across which are displayed their preference orderings of the n choice alternatives, with *occurring to the left* representing *being preferred to*.) S is a *circular matrix*: each row is derived from its predecessor by a circular permutation; and each element in turn heads a row, then in every other row it follows the element that heads the next row.

Letting "$\alpha \to \beta$" represent the claim that α is preferred by all but one of the voters to β, setting S contains the following $\to$ cycle:

$$c_1 \to c_2 \to \ldots \to c_i \to c_j \to \ldots \to c_{m-1} \to c_m \to c_1$$

Replacing each occurrence of c_1 in S by the ordered pair $\langle x, y \rangle$, we get maximal setting T.

$$T = \begin{array}{c} v_1: \\ v_2: \\ v_3: \\ \vdots \\ v_m: \end{array} \begin{bmatrix} x & y & c_2 & \cdots & \cdots & c_m \\ c_m & x & y & c_2 & \cdots & c_{m-1} \\ c_{m-1} & c_m & x & y & c_2 & \cdots \\ & & & & & \vdots \\ c_2 & \cdots & c_{m-1} & c_m & x & y \end{bmatrix}$$

Still letting "$\to$" represent *being preferred to by all but one of the voters*, setting T contains the following $\to$ chain:

$$y \to c_2 \to \ldots \to c_i \to c_j \to \ldots \to c_{m-1} \to c_m \to x$$

Notice that every voter in T prefers x to y.

We will now derive a contradiction from the assumption

that a device satisfies both (U) and (P) and is not vicious. By unlimited scope a device must accept maximal setting T, and to avoid being vicious in T it cannot socially rank x above c_m, c_m above c_{m-1}, . . ., c_j above c_i, . . ., or c_2 above y, since for each contiguous pair α and β, one voter prefers α to β while all other voters have the opposite preference. By connectedness, if α is not preferred to β, then either β is preferred to α or β and α are indifferent. Letting R represent social preference-or-indifference, in setting T we have

$$Ryc_2, \ldots, Rc_ic_j, \ldots, Rc_mx$$

Assuming this R-chain finite, transitivity of R yields Ryx in setting T. This means that y is socially preferred-or-indifferent to x, which implies that x is not socially preferred to y. But this violates the Pareto principle, since everybody in setting T prefers x to y. Therefore, any device that satisfies (U) and (P) must be vicious. Q.E.D.

Lemma 2. Any vicious device that satisfies (U), (P), (PA), and (I) must be dictatorial.

Proof. Let "W" represent the complex relation that holds between a pair of alternatives x and y when there is an individual K in a maximal setting, such that K prefers x to y, all other voters prefer y to x, and some device ranks x socially preferred to y. Let "D" represent the complex relation that holds between a pair of alternatives x and y when there is an individual K such that in every setting where K prefers x to y, a device ranks x socially preferred to y. Then for any aggregation device AD satisfying (U), (P), (PA), and (I), and any individual K, the following three statements hold.

1. For any alternatives x and y, if AD ranks x socially preferred to y in every setting where K prefers x to y, then

107

AD ranks x socially preferred to y in some maximal setting where K prefers x to y and all other voters prefer y to x [that is, $(x)(y)(Dxy \supset Wxy)$].

2. For any alternatives x, y, and z, if there is a maximal setting in which K prefers x to y, all other voters prefer y to x, and AD ranks x socially preferred to y, then AD ranks x socially preferred to z in every setting in which K prefers x to z [that is, $(x)(y)(z)(Wxy \supset Dxz)$].

3. For any alternatives x, y, and z, if there is a maximal setting in which K prefers x to y, all other voters prefer y to x, and AD ranks x socially preferred to y, then AD ranks z socially preferred to y in every setting in which K prefers z to y [that is, $(x)(y)(z)(Wxy \supset Dzy)$].

We shall establish these three claims shortly, but for now note that they have as a consequence,

C. If there is a maximal setting in which AD ranks x socially preferred to y when K prefers x to y and all other voters prefer y to x, then for every pair of alternatives u and v, AD ranks u socially preferred to v in every setting in which K prefers u to v [that is, $(\exists x)(\exists y)Wxy \supset (u)(v)Duv$].

Consequence C, of course, is what we want to prove: that a vicious device which satisfies (U), (P), (PA), and (I) is dictatorial. Its derivation from premises 1 through 3 is a straightforward matter of elementary predicate logic which we will do as soon as we establish the three premises.

Premise 1 is obvious. If AD's social ranking of x and y duplicates K's preference in every setting where K prefers x to y, it does so in the special case of a maximal setting where K prefers x to y and all other voters prefer y to x.

Premise 2 is established as follows. Suppose that there is a maximal setting M in which K prefers x to y, all other voters prefer y to x, AD ranks x socially preferred to y, and yet there is a setting Q where K prefers x to z but AD does not rank x socially preferred to z. Now consider setting R which differs from Q only, if at all, in that K prefers x to y, all other voters prefer y to x, everybody (K included) prefers y to z, K prefers x to z, and all other voters prefer x and z however they do in Q. Either setting R is maximal or it is not.

i. If R is maximal, then since maximal settings contain all the voters there are, all individual preferences toward x and y are identical in settings R and M. So, by condition (I), x and y must be socially ranked the same in R as they were in M: x socially preferred to y.

ii. If R is not maximal, then it has fewer voters than M. K and all the voters it does contain have the same preferences toward x and y that they have in setting M, but M contains additional voters who prefer y to x. Thus, as far as x and y are concerned, R is equivalent to a maximal setting just like M except that those additional voters abstain. Now condition (PA) requires that if x is socially preferred to y and the only thing that changes is that some voters who previously preferred y to x cease doing so, then x not suffer vis-à-vis y in the social ranking. So since AD ranks x socially preferred to y in M, it must continue to do so in R.

Therefore, no matter whether R is maximal or not, AD ranks x socially preferred to y. And since everybody in R prefers y to z, condition (P) requires that AD rank y socially preferred to z. So, by transitivity, AD ranks x socially preferred to z in setting R. But, by hypothesis, all individual preferences toward x and z are identical in settings R and Q. Hence, condition (I) makes AD rank them the same in Q as in R: x socially preferred to z. So, given that there is a maximal setting where K prefers x to y, all other voters prefer y to x, and AD ranks x socially preferred to y, there cannot be a setting in which K prefers x to z and yet AD does not rank x socially preferred to z.

Premise 3 is established by an appropriate adaptation of the argument for premise 2. Let there be a maximal setting M where K prefers x to y, all other voters prefer y to x, AD ranks x socially preferred to y, and yet there is a setting U where K prefers z to y but AD does not rank z socially preferred to y. Now consider setting V, which differs from U only, if at all, in that K prefers x

to y, all other voters prefer y to x, everybody (K included) prefers z to x, K prefers z to y, and all other voters prefer z and y however they do in U. Again, either V is maximal or it is not.

  i. If V is maximal, then for the same reason as before, AD ranks x socially preferred to y.
  ii. If V is not maximal, then for the same reason as before, AD ranks x socially preferred to y.

So either way, AD ranks x socially preferred to y. And since everybody in V prefers z to x, condition (P) requires that AD rank z socially preferred to x. So, by transitivity, AD ranks z socially preferred to y. Again, by hypothesis, all individual preferences toward z and y are identical in settings U and V. So condition (I) makes AD rank them the same in U as in V: z socially preferred to y. Therefore, given that there is a maximal setting where K prefers x to y, all other voters prefer y to x, and AD ranks x socially preferred to y, there cannot be a setting in which K prefers z to y and yet AD does not rank z socially preferred to y.

  It only remains to set out the derivation of consequence C from premises 1 through 3.

1.	$(x)(y)(Dxy \supset Wxy)$	Premise
2.	$(x)(y)(z)(Wxy \supset Dxz)$	Premise
3.	$(x)(y)(z)(Wxy \supset Dzy)$	Premise
4.	$(\exists x)(\exists y)Wxy$	Conditional Proof Assumption
5.	Wab	4 E.I.
6.	$Wab \supset Dav$	2 U.I.
7.	$Dav \supset Wav$	1 U.I.
8.	$Wav \supset Duv$	3 U.I.
9.	Duv	5–8 Tautology
10.	$(u)(v)Duv$	9 U.G.
C.	$(\exists x)(\exists y)Wxy \supset$ $(u)(v)Duv$	4–10 Conditional Proof

Q.E.D.

Since we have established premises 1 through 3 and shown consequence C to follow deductively therefrom, we have established consequence C. So any vicious device that satisfies (U), (P), (PA), and (I) is dictatorial, which completes our proof of lemma 2.

But we saw in lemma 1 that satisfying (U) and (P) implies that a device is vicious. So from lemmas 1 and 2 it follows that no device can jointly satisfy conditions (U), (P), (PA), (D), and (I), given that preference and indifference are logically well-behaved. This completes the proof of our version of Arrow's Theorem.[2]

2. The reader is invited to compare Arrow's original proof [*Social Choice and Individual Values* (New York: John Wiley & Sons, 1951), chap. 5, sec. 3] and his later version [2d ed. (New Haven, Conn.: Yale University Press, 1963), chap. 8, sec. 2].

7

Impossibility and Infinity

With Arrow's Theorem now finally before us, let us pick up the discussion where we left it. We were considering "ways out" which infringe condition (U), unlimited scope, for instance, single-peakedness, the requirement that in every admissible triple of candidates there be at least one that all voters agree is not worst. The problem is to find an independent way of motivating such restrictions, given the (defeasible) presumption in favor of unlimited scope. As we noted in earlier discussions, situations where voters view candidates as falling on the left–center–right spectrum provide plausible instances of single-peaked settings. But such intuitive plausibility seems insufficient to rebut the standing presumption in favor of unlimited scope. Now we shall try a different approach, which, if successful, will provide that independent motivation by offering a new framework for thinking about these matters. Also, it will speak to our original project of explaining Arrow's result and removing the air of paradox. And since we recently added a further desideratum—that our explanation of Arrow's paradox also, and uniformly, deal with the paradoxes of majority voting—for good measure it will do that too.

Our new approach will involve showing how both Arrow's result and the paradoxes of majority voting contain instances of an ancient, familiar philosophical strategy, viz. the *infinite regress argument*. Following that we will show how accepting pattern restrictions like single-peakedness can be comparable to positing a (preferential) first cause, the traditional remedy for a regress.

A famous classical instance of an infinite regress argument is this.

> It is certain, and evident to our senses, that in the world some things are in motion. . . . Whatever is in motion must be put in motion by another. If that by which it is put in motion be itself put in motion, then this also must needs be put in motion by another, and that by another again. But this cannot go on to infinity, because then there would be no first mover, and consequently, no other mover. . . . Therefore, it is necessary to arrive at a first mover, put in motion by no other. . . .[1]

The following is a contemporary instance of the same form.

> There must be some intuitive beliefs if any beliefs are to be justified at all. By an intuitive belief is meant one which does not owe its truth or credibility to some other belief or beliefs from which it can be inferred. For a belief to be justified it is not enough for it to be accepted, let alone merely entertained. There must also be good reason for accepting it. Certainly some beliefs are justifiable by reference to others, but only if these other beliefs are themselves established or well confirmed. If every belief was dependent on others for its justification, no belief would be justified at all, for in this case to justify any belief would require the justification of an infinite series of beliefs. So if any belief is to be justified there must be a class of basic, non-inferential beliefs to bring the regress of justification to a halt.[2]

1. St. Thomas Aquinas, *Summa Theologica*, Part I, Q. 2, art. 3.
2. Anthony Quinton, "The Foundations of Knowledge," in B. Williams and A. Montefiori, eds., *British Analytical Philosophy* (Atlantic Highlands, N.J.: Humanities Press, 1966), p. 58.

Impossibility and Infinity

The argument in both cases proceeds by assuming some plausible characteristics (like transitivity, asymmetry, and so forth) about an important or interesting binary relation—*putting in motion, being evidence for*—and deducing therefrom a vicious infinite regress, the unacceptability of which establishes the existence of (or at least, the need for) something to block the regress—a prime mover, the foundations of knowledge. The argument really moves in two stages: the first being the deducing of the regress; the second, the positing of the remedy. The first stage, as we shall see, can be reversed; and when run backward, as it were—assuming finitude (the negation of the normal first-stage conclusion) plus all but one (say, transitivity) of the other plausible characteristics—can be used to argue the nontransitivity of the relation in question. It is a maneuver like this that occurs in Arrow's result and in the paradoxes of majority voting. Seeing this removes the paradoxical sting from these results by placing them in familiar argument-strategic surroundings.[3]

3. Students of the infinite regress argument find it in unlikely places. The mathematician E. W. Beth discusses what he calls Aristotle's Principle of the Absolute: $(\exists u)(\exists v)Fuv \supset (\exists f)(x)((x \neq f) \supset (Fxf \,\&\, \sim Ffx))$ (that is, If anything stands in the F relation, then something has F to everything else, and nothing else has F to it). The entity f (which thus blocks the regress) Beth calls "the absolute entity corresponding to the relation F." He lists the following applications of the Principle of the Absolute:

    (1) Let Fxy be the phrase: x takes its origin from y; then f will be the *principle* (ἀρχή) in the sense of pre-Socratic philosophy.

    (2) Let Fxy be the phrase: x *is moved by* y; then f will be the *Prime Mover* in the sense of Aristotle.

    (3) Let Fxy be the phrase: x *is desired for the sake of* y: then f will be the *summum bonum* in the sense of Aristotle. . . .

    (4) Let Fxy be the phrase: *the truth* (or *the notion*) x *presupposes the truth* (or *the notion*) y; then f will be the *principle* in the sense of Aristotle's theory of science. . . .

    (5) Let Fxy be the phrase: x *is in a certain state of movement with regard to* y; then f will be Newton's *absolute space*.

I. The Structure of the Infinite Regress Argument

For our structural analysis we rely on the lucid account in David H. Sanford's "Infinity and Vagueness,"[4] the relevant portion of which follows:

> So long as "R" is interpreted in the same way throughout, any five statements of the following forms are mutually inconsistent:
>
> (1) *Existence.* $(\exists x)(\exists y)Rxy$
> Something exists which has relation R to something.
>
> (2) *Asymmetry.* $(x)(y)(Rxy \supset \sim Ryx)$
> If x has R to y, then y does not have R to x.
>
> (3) *Transitivity.* $(x)(y)(z)((Rxy \ \& \ Ryz) \supset Rxz)$
> If x has R to y which in turn has R to z, then x has R to z.
>
> (4) *Existential Heredity.* $(x)(y)(Rxy \supset (\exists z)Rzx)$
> If x has R to y, then something has R to x.
>
> (5) *Finitude.* There are only finitely many things related by relation R.

Since the five statements are mutually inconsistent, the falsity of any one follows from the truth of the other four. In most cases where the argument is used, the suppositions of existence, asymmetry, and transitivity are beyond question, so either the assumption of existential heredity or the assumption of finitude must be rejected. If the assumption of heredity is true, then there are infinitely many things related by R. If there are not infinitely many things related by R, then the assumption of heredity is false and there is something which has R to something else but to which nothing has R.[5]

> (6) Let Fxy be the phrase: *the imperative x is based on the imperative y;* then f will be the *categorical imperative* in the sense of Kant.
>
> (7) Let Fxy be the phrase: *x takes its exchange value from y;* then f will be the *Wertsubstanz* in the sense of Marx.

[E. W. Beth, *The Foundations of Mathematics* (Amsterdam: North-Holland, 1959), pp. 9–11.]

4. *The Philosophical Review* 84 (October 1975): 520–35.
5. Ibid., pp. 520–21. The inconsistency is proved on pp. 534–35.

Impossibility and Infinity

Intuitively, here is how the infinite regress argument works. The key element is existential heredity (or just heredity, for short). It is the driving force behind the regress, the other four elements merely ensuring (a) that it gets started, and (b) that it does not get diverted into a circle. Heredity says,

> If anything has R to something, something else has R to it. (That is, nothing has R to anything without something else having R to it.)

This obviously has powerful regress generating potential, but there are at least the following ways it can fail to induce a regress:

A. If nothing has R to anything, and
B. If R related things form a circle, which can happen
   (i) If a thing has R to itself—a degenerate circle,
   (ii) If two things have R to each other—a tight circle, or
   (iii) If more than two things form a closed, R-cycle, for example,

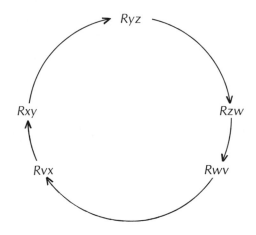

The function of existence is to rule out A, of asymmetry to rule out B(i) and B(ii), and of transitivity to rule out B(iii) (with the help of asymmetry). Thus, existence trivially falsifies A. By asymmetry, if a thing has R to itself, then it does not have R to itself, a contradiction that falsifies B(i). Asymmetry obviously falsifies B(ii). And here is how transitivity (plus asymmetry) falsifies B(iii). Consider the finite R-cycle above. From Rxy and Ryz, transitivity yields Rxz. From that and Rzw, transitivity yields Rxw. And from that and Rwv, transitivity yields Rxv. But asymmetry prohibits both Rxv and Rvx from occurring together. So what transitivity does is "collapse" finite R-cycles into two-element R-cycles, which asymmetry dispatches.

As Sanford remarks, most traditional uses of the argument assume the first three characteristics (existence, asymmetry, and transitivity) and pit heredity, whose denial implies a first cause, against finitude, whose denial implies a vicious regress. But as he also notes, the falsity of any one of the five can be deduced from the truth of the other four. Thus, from existence, asymmetry, heredity, and finitude one can deduce non-transitivity. And from existence, heredity, transitivity, and finitude one can deduce nonasymmetry. And so on. In the next section we will argue that the paradoxes of majority voting can be viewed in this way. They are applications of infinite regress arguments in which we establish four of these characteristics about the binary relation *social preference*, and deduce from that the denial of the fifth.

II. Majority Voting and the Infinite Regress Argument

The central idea behind majority rule is this: when a candidate x is preferred to another y by a majority of voters in a setting, a majoritarian aggregation device must rank x above y in its social ranking. In our schematic reconstruction of the infinite regress argument, let Rxy be: x *is socially preferred to* y, and let this be determined by majority voting. Now consider the para-

117

dox of voting. This, it will be recalled, is a setting containing three candidates (A, B, C) and three voters (v_1, v_2, v_3) such that v_1 prefers A to B to C, v_2 prefers C to A to B, and v_3 prefers B to C to A. In this setting, existence of R is satisfied since something is preferred by a majority to something else. And finitude holds since there are only three candidates in the setting. Moreover, heredity is satisfied since for every candidate preferred to another by a majority, there is a candidate preferred to it by a majority Finally, given the nature of majorities, R is asymmetric: if a majority prefers x to y, a majority does not prefer y to x. By the infinite regress argument, if a binary relation R is asymmetric and satisfies existence, heredity, and finitude, it cannot be transitive. So majority voting does not always yield transitive results.

Put another way, the infinite regress argument shows that if social preference is to be both asymmetric and transitive, then we cannot admit finite settings whose patterns of individual preferences make (majoritarian) social preference hereditary. Thus, built into this way of putting it is a (potential) infringement of unlimited scope. Should a finite setting have a preference pattern that makes majoritarian social preference hereditary, it will be inadmissible. This is a (potential) pattern restriction. (Furthermore, if a majoritarian device also satisfies independence of irrelevant alternatives, the pattern restriction applies not only to admissible settings, but to all triples of candidates in admissible settings. No admissible triple of candidates can exhibit a pattern of individual preferences which (in conjunction with majority rule) makes social preference hereditary *for that triple*.)

This, then, shows how the paradoxes of majority voting can be viewed as applications of the infinite regress argument. The general moral is this. If a social preference relation is to be asymmetric and transitive, then, for a given device, no finite setting can be admitted whose pattern of individual preferences

118

would make the relation hereditary, given the nature of the device. This general moral will specify different particular pattern restrictions, depending on the nature of the device in question. For a majoritarian device it will rule out settings such as the paradox of voting. As we will show shortly, for a device that satisfies both the Pareto principle and nonviciousness, it will rule out settings such as maximal setting T (in lemma 1 of our proof of Arrow's Theorem). And in general, for a device of nature N, it will rule out settings whose preference patterns conjoin with N-constraints to make the social preference relation in question hereditary. The general moral is obviously a social-choice adaptation of an infinite regress argument. It exploits the familiar joint incompatibility of existence, asymmetry, transitivity, finitude, and heredity by assuming the first four and deducing therefrom (its version of) the denial of the fifth. Next we shall see that one social-choice response to the paradox—the "built-in" pattern restriction dictated by the general moral—functions just like the traditional remedy for the regress, positing a first cause.

Single-peakedness is a pattern restriction which requires that in order for a triple of candidates to be admissible it must contain at least one candidate that all voters agree is not worst. This prevents majoritarian social preference from being hereditary, as the following shows. Assume the contrary. Suppose a triple of candidates, x, y, z, did contain one that all voters agreed not to be worst, and assume that majoritarian social preference was hereditary for that triple. If all voters agree that one candidate is not worst, then that candidate does not occur last in any voter's preference. But if majoritarian social preference is hereditary in that triple, then a majority of voters prefers x to y, a majority prefers y to z, and a majority prefers z to x. Now this cannot happen without some candidate occupying the bottom of some voter's list. Because if more than half prefer a to b, and more than half prefer b to c, then at least one voter must both prefer a

to *b* and *b* to *c*. Then, given transitivity of individual preference, that voter prefers *a* to *b* to *c*, and candidate *c* occurs last in his preference list. Since this reasoning holds equally for each of the three candidates, it follows that in order to be hereditary in a given triple, majoritarian social preference requires a pattern of individual preferences in which each candidate occurs last in at least one voter's preferences. So single-peakedness, by preventing *that* in every admissible triple, prevents majoritarian social preference from being hereditary. Thus, it does indirectly what positing a (preferential) first cause does directly: it rules out just the settings that would make majoritarian social preference hereditary.

A majoritarian "first cause" would be a candidate, *x*, preferred to another candidate, *y*, by a majority of the voters in a setting where no candidate was preferred to *x* by a majority. Requiring that every admissible setting—or, in view of condition (I), every admissible triple of candidates—contain such a first cause candidate trivially guarantees that majoritarian social preference cannot be hereditary. Because heredity requires precisely that for every candidate preferred to another by a majority, there be a candidate preferred to it by a majority, a requirement that the existence of a majoritarian first cause explicitly contradicts. Thus single-peakedness and a majoritarian first cause both restrict the scope of a majoritarian device to settings whose patterns of individual preferences do not (in conjunction with majority rule) make social preference hereditary. They both infringe unlimited scope in order to block the regress.

We might have cast this all as an "impossibility result": that no majoritarian device can have unlimited scope if social preference is both asymmetric and transitive. Why does it help to put it instead in this other way, as an infinite regress argument? Perhaps only because the latter strategy is so utterly familiar. Long use has accustomed us to see the connection between its premises, and to feel the naturalness of drawing its conclusion. After more than 2000 years, it is hard to feel that positing a first cause is an unnatural, arbitrary, or ad hoc way out of an infinite regress. In the causal application, for instance, it is plain that (given the other premises) finitude is hostage to heredity. We can just "see" the finite circle of things causing things causing things . . . bending back upon itself unacceptably, unless there is something which causes but is not caused. Here is no paradox, no feeling that each of the operative conditions is "so different in substance as not to permit interaction of any kind." Yet the facts here are, in a sense, just the ones we originally found puzzling about Arrow's Theorem. All the conditions are logically independent; no one bears any logical relation to any other, neither contradicting nor implying it. The five taken together are inconsistent, but no subset is. Yet we "see" the infinite regress argument as natural, normal, and familiar; but Arrow's Theorem as puzzling and paradoxical.

Perhaps the reason is this. With the infinite regress argument we have the ability to assume most of the conditions as background, and "see" the remainder as related conditional upon those assumptions. Heredity and finitude, for example, are quite independent when considered by themselves, merely as characteristics of binary relations. But they are easily seen to be "conditional contraries"—the truth of either implies the falsity of the other, *conditional upon* the relation in question's also satisfying existence, asymmetry, and transitivity. Very likely it is this seeing conditional connections, connections between things which only emerge upon assuming other things, which makes the infinite regress argument seem so unexceptionable. Whatever the reason, we will try to exploit it by finding a way to "see" Arrow's Theorem itself as containing an application of the infinite regress argument.

III. Arrow's Theorem and the Infinite Regress Argument

Recall that our proof strategy in chapter 6 was first to establish a restricted version of the result—showing in lemma 1 that no device could meet conditions (U) and (P) without being vicious—then, in lemma 2, to extend this limited "paradox" to full generality. We will now show how lemma 1, the paradoxical "core" of the fully general result, embodies an application of the infinite regress argument. In outline, our proof of lemma 1 was this. We let R represent *social preference-or-indifference*, and P represent (strict) *social preference*. ["(P)" stands for the Pareto principle.]

1. By condition (U), maximal setting T is admissible.

$$T = \begin{array}{c} v_1: \\ v_2: \\ v_3: \\ \vdots \\ v_m: \end{array} \left[\begin{array}{cccccc} x & y & c_2 & \cdots & \cdots & c_m \\ c_m & x & y & c_2 & \cdots & c_{m-1} \\ c_{m-1} & c_m & x & y & c_2 & \cdots \\ \vdots & \vdots & & & & \vdots \\ c_2 & \cdots & c_{m-1} & c_m & x & y \end{array} \right]$$

2. By nonviciousness (Non-V), we have the following R-chain: $Ryc_2, \ldots, Rc_ic_j, \ldots, Rc_mx$. Assuming this chain finite,
3. by transitivity of R, Ryx. But
4. by condition (P), Pxy since everybody in T prefers x to y. Now
5. Pxy implies not Ryx. Therefore,
6. No device can jointly satisfy (U), (P), and (Non-V). Q.E.D.

To see the infinite regress argument here, notice that from the same facts we could equally well have concluded,

7. If a device with unlimited scope satisfies both (P) and (Non-V), there must be an admissible finite setting in which R is not transitive.

Or again, we could have concluded,

8. If a device satisfies both (P) and (Non-V), and if R is transitive, then not every admissible setting can be finite.

Finally, to establish the parallel with our treatment of majority voting, we could have concluded,

9. If R is to be transitive, then we cannot admit any finite setting whose pattern of individual preferences [in conjunction with (P) and (Non-V)] makes it hereditary.

The parallel fails to be perfect, in a way we will discuss shortly,
but even so there is recognizably a version of the infinite regress
argument at work here. It points, as before, to an infringement of
unlimited scope as the natural way out. And, as before, accepting such a pattern restriction is comparable to positing a first
cause, the standard remedy for a regress.

Here's how the parallel fails. In contrast with our treatment of
majority voting, the key relation here, *social preference-or-
indifference*, is not asymmetric. So the lemma 1 situation is not
exactly parallel with that of majority voting, because there the
regress generating relation (*social preference*) is asymmetric.
Which is to say that the lemma 1 situation is not a strict instance
of the classical infinite regress argument structure. But a close
look shows that the contribution asymmetry makes to the classical argument is supplied by other features of the lemma 1 setting. So we do have something equivalent to an infinite regress
argument here, notwithstanding the one point of disanalogy.

In its pure, classical form, a social-choice application of the
infinite regress argument goes like this. Suppose there is a social
preference relation Q, satisfying all five classical regress generating conditions (including asymmetry) in some setting W.
Then W must contain an infinite number of candidates, because
(i) existence, heredity, and asymmetry of Q together imply that W
contains at least a three-element Q-string: $Qxy, Qyz, . . .$; and (ii)
if there were only finitely many candidates in W, then that
Q-string would have to form a circle; but (iii) transitivity of Q
would collapse a finite Q-circle into a two-element circle: $Qxy,
Qyx$, which would violate the asymmetry of Q. Therefore, W
must contain an infinite number of candidates in order that the
Q-string: $Qxy, Qyz, . . .$ can extend indefinitely, never forming a
finite circle, yet always allowing that for any candidate having Q

123

to another, there is another with Q to it. Only thus can transitivity be prevented from collapsing the Q-string into an asymmetry prohibited two-element circle.

Even though R (social preference-or-indifference) is not asymmetric, basically the same argument applies, given the other special features of the lemma 1 situation. Compare:

Setting T must be infinitely large, because (i) given the pattern of individual preferences in T, (Non-V) generates the extended R-string $Ryc_2, \ldots, Rc_ic_j, \ldots, Rc_mx$; and (ii) if there were only finitely many elements in the R-string, then (iii) transitivity of R would collapse it into the two-element string, Ryx, which would violate the Pareto principle, since every voter in T prefers x to y. Therefore, given its pattern of individual preferences, T must contain an infinite number of candidates in order that the R-string $Ryc_2, \ldots, Rc_ic_j, \ldots, Rc_mx$ can extend indefinitely. (The string here continually expands from the middle, as it were, rather than from either end, but the principle is the same.) Only thus can transitivity be prevented from collapsing the R-string into the Pareto-prohibited Ryx. What prevents the (transitivity collapsed) two-element string (circle) is different in the two cases: for Q it is asymmetry, for R the Pareto principle. But at bottom the arguments are the same.

Thus, in Arrow's Theorem, just as in the paradoxes of majority voting, there is a version of an infinite regress argument which points to infringing unlimited scope as the natural way out. Accepting single-peakedness turns out, again, to be a way of blocking the regress.

IV. Concluding Comment

Roughly speaking, a preference cycle can be viewed as an infinite regress diverted into a (finite) circle. The logical engine that drives the regress—whether or not it is permitted to proceed indefinitely—is existential heredity. In the theory of social choice, assuming only finite numbers of candidates, the consequence of existential heredity is preference cycles. Aristotle's response to the infinite regress, positing a first cause, was a way of denying existential heredity. In the theory of social choice, a comparable[6] strategy involves embracing pattern restrictions and violating unlimited scope. This, the preferential equivalent of positing a first cause, is the price traditionally paid to avoid a vicious regress.

In chapter 2 we dismissed this "way out" of Arrow's paradox—accepting pattern restrictions and violating Unlimited Scope—not as unthinkable, but as unmotivated and ad hoc. Now, however, having seen that Arrow's Theorem contains an infinite regress argument, and hence that accepting pattern restrictions is comparable to positing a first cause, that charge is less telling. One could hardly call positing a first cause in response to an infinite regress "unmotivated and ad hoc." Further, this provides the desired uniformity of treatment for both Arrow's paradox and the paradoxes of majority voting.

6. Comparable in certain respects (logically), not in others (ontologically). Traditionally, the infinite regress argument aims to "prove" that a first cause exists; whereas, the paradox of voting, say, does not aim to "prove" that a majority candidate exists. We wish to emphasize the logico-argumentative similarities of requiring single-peakedness and positing a first cause, without gainsaying the different epistemological and ontological points of employing these strategies. I thank Russell Hardin for pointing out the need for this clarification.

Afterword

In the beginning we hoped to find a way of understanding Arrow's impossibility theorem which would remove (or anyway, lessen) its air of paradox. Initially, it presented a puzzling case of conceptual action-at-a-distance: the four "rationality" conditions, each independently plausible, together demonstrably inconsistent, with no apparent connections through which either influence or obstruction could flow. A considerable part of our early labors (chapters 1 through 4) involved doing what is rightly expected of philosophers, namely, scrutinizing the axioms: exploring their implications, arguing pros and cons, formulating (if not deciding) crucial issues; in short, exposition, analysis, and clarification.

We then (in chapter 5) began examining some possible "ways out," in the course of which we developed an additional aim: that whatever strategy we offered for resolving Arrow's paradox also, and uniformly, handle the paradoxes of majority voting. In chapter 6 we proved a version of Arrow's Theorem.

In chapter 7 we developed a new approach, showing how both Arrow's Theorem and the paradoxes of majority voting could be viewed as applications of an old familiar philosophical strategy, the infinite regress argument. This was our explanation, designed to induce a recognitional gestalt which would dispel the air of paradox. The idea was that the infinite regress argument, being so overwhelmingly normal, natural, and familiar, would defeat and neutralize any suggestion of strangeness or paradox in any argument that could be assimilated to it. Following from this we nominated Arrow's condition (U), unlimited scope, as most eligible for infringement. Accepting pattern restrictions, we argued, is comparable to positing a first cause, the traditional way out of an infinite regress.

No doubt this "explanation" will not work for everyone. Understanding, of the sort we are after, is personality or mind set, perhaps temperament-relative. It is all a question of coming to "see" a puzzling phenomenon as comfortably familiar. Seeing an infinite regress argument at work in Arrow's Theorem and in the paradoxes of majority voting is, hopefully, one way of doing that, for some people. For others, perhaps our account will serve as a target, or maybe a foil, against which alternative, competing accounts can be developed. The more the better. They cannot but enhance our understanding.

Appendix

We will now present some results[1] on preference cycles, circular matrices, and a phenomenon we call *preference anarchy*. Since preference cycles of one sort or another are at the heart of most of the paradoxes of social choice, these results may be of interest to mathematically inclined readers. They bear independently on our recommendation that the paradoxes be avoided by not admitting settings containing circular matrices (strictly, settings containing patterns of individual preferences which can be associated with circular matrices). And in a certain sense they explain why, for example, majoritarian social preference is hereditary in the paradox of voting.

I. The Main Theorem

We will use the following technical terms.

T.1 A setting is *standard* if all voters have preferences toward all candidates, and their preferences are all strict, linear orderings.

T.2 A setting is *normal* if it contains no fewer voters than candidates.

1. The mathematical results presented here were worked out jointly by the author and Edward T. Wong of the Department of Mathematics, Oberlin College.

T.3 Candidate c_i has a *simple coalition* against candidate c_j if and only if at least two voters prefer c_i to c_j.

T.4 A *coalition candidate* has simple coalitions against every other candidate.

T.5 A setting is *anarchic* when it contains no coalition candidate.

T.6 Candidate c_i has a *majority coalition* against candidate c_j if and only if at least a majority of voters prefer c_i to c_j.

T.7 A *majority candidate* has majority coalitions against every other candidate.

Inspection reveals that the paradox of voting is a normal, standard, anarchic setting. We will show how this requires that majority preference be cyclical. We start by characterizing the preceding notions more rigorously.

The system we shall study consists of two finite sets V and C of m and n elements, respectively. The elements of V are voters and of C candidates. To each voter v_i, the system associates a linearly ordered preference chain, $c_{i,1} > c_{i,2} > \cdots > c_{i,n}$, where the $c_{i,j}$ are candidates and the "$>$" represents strict preference. In the notation $c_{i,j}$ the first subscript indicates which voter's preference chain the candidate appears in (voter v_i), the second subscript indicates which position it has in that chain (position j). This amounts to row/column specification in a matrix.

If C' is a subset of C, then for any voter v_i, a linearly ordered preference chain of v_i with respect to C' can be obtained by deleting the elements in the chain of v_i in C which are not in C'. We call $\{V', C'\}$ a *subsystem* if V' and C' are subsets of V and C, respectively, and the linearly ordered preference chains of elements of V' in C' are obtained by deletion in the manner specified.

If $(v_1, \ldots, v_m)$ is an ordered set of voters in V, we can associate the system with an $m \times n$ matrix

$$(C_{i,j}) = \begin{bmatrix} c_{1,1} & c_{1,2} & \cdots & c_{1,n} \\ c_{i,1} & c_{i,2} & \cdots & c_{i,n} \\ c_{m,1} & c_{m,2} & \cdots & c_{m,n} \end{bmatrix}$$

where the ith row of $(C_{i,j})$ is the chain of v_i in C. Clearly, any matrix of the system can be obtained by interchanging rows from a given matrix.

For any two candidates c_i, c_j in C, we let $N(c_i, c_j)$ be the number of voters in V who prefer c_i to c_j (that is, the number of voters v_k where $c_i > c_j$ in the chain of v_k in C). Thus, where m is the number of voters in V, $0 \leq N(c_i,c_j) \leq m$, and $N(c_j, c_i) = m - N(c_i, c_j)$ if $c_i \neq c_j$ and the system is standard.

A candidate c_i is a *coalition candidate* if $N(c_i, c_j) \geq 2$ for all $c_j \neq c_i$.

A system is *anarchic* if it has no coalition candidate. Hence, for each candidate c_i in an anarchic system there is at least one candidate $c_j \neq c_i$ such that $N(c_j, c_i) \geq m - 1$.

A candidate c_i is a *majority candidate* if $N(c_i, c_j) > [m/2]$, where $[m/2]$ is the largest integer $\leq m/2$, for all $c_j \neq c_i$.

A system lacks a majority candidate if and only if for each candidate c_i there is a candidate $c_j \neq c_i$ such that $N(c_j, c_i) \geq [m/2]$.

Finally, a system is *normal* if the number of voters m, is not less than the number of candidates n.

Theorem 1. If a normal, standard system is anarchic, then the elements in each column of any matrix of the system are distinct. Consequently, any matrix of the system must be square (that is, the number of voters = the number of candidates).

Proof. Let $(C_{i,j})$ be a matrix of such a system. If there were two identical elements in the first column, then, since each first-column candidate defeats every other candidate in its row (and all candidates occur in each row), the candidate with two first-column occurrences would be a coalition candidate, and the system would not be anarchic. So all the elements in the first column are distinct. By normalcy, the number of voters (rows) m is not less than the number of candidates (columns) n. But m cannot be greater than n, or else some candidate would need double occurrence in the first column to prevent gaps. But by standardness there are no gaps. So $m = n$, and any matrix of the system must be square.

The remainder of the theorem is proved by the method of induction. We have already established (1) that all the elements in the first column are distinct. We will show (2) that for any finite k, if all the elements in each of the first k columns are distinct, then so are all the elements in column $k + 1$. Strong induction will then allow us to infer (3) that all the elements in every column are distinct. [1]

So assume that all the elements in each of the first k columns of $(C_{i,j})$ are distinct, but that there are two identical elements—call them c—in column $k + 1$. Since by hypothesis all elements in each of the first k columns are distinct, and by standardness each element occurs once in each row, and there are no gaps, there is a row in which candidate c occurs first, one in which it occurs second, one third, and so on. Hence, by interchanging rows of $(C_{i,j})$, we can obtain a matrix of the system in which, down through row k, candidate c occupies the ith position in the ith row. That is, each occurrence of c is on the main diagonal of the matrix. Likewise, by interchanging rows we can arrange matters so that the double occurrence of candidate c in column $k + 1$ yields a matrix of the system in the form on page 132. Notice that candidate c is preferred to all other candidates by voter v_1, and preferred to all others except candidate $c_{2,1}$ by voter v_2. If we can show that c is preferred to $c_{2,1}$ by any voter other than v_1 and v_2, we will have shown c to be a coalition candidate, since it will thereby have simple coalitions (at least two votes) against every other candidate. But that will contradict preference anarchy, from which we can conclude that all the elements of column $k + 1$ of the original matrix $(C_{i,j})$ must be distinct.

Focus on the interior diagonal immediately left of the main diagonal. Consider the set of elements that immediately precede occurrences of candidate c in rows 3 through $k + 1$: the set $\{c_{3,2}, c_{4,3}, \cdots, c_{k,k-1}, c_{k+1,k}\}$. Call this the *special set*. Is the special set composed exclusively of occurrences of candidate $c_{2,1}$, or does

Appendix

$$
\begin{array}{c}
v_1: \\[1.5em]
v_2: \\[2em]
\\[2em]
v_k: \\[2em]
\\[2em]
\\[2em]
v_m:
\end{array}
\left[
\begin{array}{ccccccc}
c & c_{1,2} & \cdots & \cdots & c_{1,k} & \cdots & c_{1,m} \\[1.5em]
c_{2,1} & c & \cdots & \cdots & c_{2,k} & \cdot & \cdot \\[1.5em]
c_{3,1} & c_{3,2} & \cdots & \cdots & c_{3,k} & \cdot & \cdot \\[0.5em]
\vdots & \vdots & \vdots & \vdots & \vdots & \vdots & \vdots \\[0.5em]
c_{k,1} & c_{k,2} & \cdots & c_{k,k-1} & c & \cdot & \cdot \\[1.5em]
c_{k+1,1} & \cdots & \cdots & \cdots & c_{k+1,k} & c & \cdot \\[1.5em]
c_{k+2,1} & \cdots & \cdots & \cdots & k+2,k & c & \cdot \\[0.5em]
\vdots & \vdots & \vdots & \vdots & \vdots & \vdots & \vdots \\[0.5em]
\cdots & \cdots & \cdots & \cdots & \cdots & \cdots & c_{m,m}
\end{array}
\right]
$$

it contain other candidates, different from $c_{2,1}$? Suppose the latter, and let $c_{i+1,i}$ be the first such different candidate in the special set. Since this one, occurring in column i, is the first in the special set different from $c_{2,1}$, the latter occurs in each of the first $i - 1$ columns. (That is, the interior diagonal next left of the main diagonal is composed of occurrences of $c_{2,1}$ at least to its intersection with column $i - 1$.) But this means that $c_{2,1}$ must occur to the right of candidate c in row $i + 1$. Because, by the inductive hypothesis, all the elements in the first k columns are distinct. So $c_{2,1}$ cannot occur in row $i + 1$ in positions 1 through i. It occurs in position 1 in row 2, and in positions 2 through $i - 1$ in the special set; so since it does not have double occurrences in any column, it cannot occur in row $i + 1$ in any of those positions. Nor can it occur there in position i itself, since that position contains the first element of the special set different from $c_{2,1}$. But, by standardness, each candidate occurs in each

132

row, so it must occur somewhere in row $i + 1$. So it occurs to the right of candidate c in that row. But that means that voter v_{i+1} prefers c to $c_{2,1}$, and hence candidate c is a coalition candidate. Since this contradicts preference anarchy, we conclude that our special set contains nothing but occurrences of $c_{2,1}$. Which is to say, $c_{2,1} = c_{3,2} = \ldots = c_{k,k-1} = c_{k+1,k}$.

But in this case, $c_{2,1}$ must occur to the right of candidate c in row $k + 2$. Because, by the same reasoning as before, it cannot occur in row $k + 2$ in positions 1 through k (since all those positions are occupied in our special set by occurrences of $c_{2,1}$ already, and by the inductive hypothesis it does not have double occurrence in the first k columns). Nor can it occur there in position $k + 1$, since that position is occupied by one of the double occurrences of candidate c. So it must occur to the right of c in that row. So voter v_{k+2} prefers c to $c_{2,1}$ and c is a coalition candidate. Since this contradicts preference anarchy, all the elements of column $k + 1$ of the original matrix $(C_{i,j})$ must be distinct. So, by induction, all the elements of all its columns are distinct. Q.E.D.

Still assuming the system to be normal, standard, and anarchic, let c_1 be any candidate in C and choose voters $v_1, v_2, \ldots, v_m$ in V where c_1 appears in the ith position in the chain of v_i. Also, let $c_{m-(i-2)}$ be the element that appears in the first position in the chain of v_i, $i = 2, \ldots, m$. The matrix of the system in this arrangement is of the following form:

$$(C_{i,j}) = \begin{bmatrix} c_1 & c_{1,2} & \cdots & \cdots & c_{1,m} \\ c_m & c_1 & \cdots & \cdots & c_{2,m} \\ \vdots & \vdots & & \vdots & \vdots \\ c_3 & c_{m-1,2} & \cdots & c_1 & c_{m-1,m} \\ c_2 & c_{m,2} & \cdots & c_{m,m-1} & c_1 \end{bmatrix}$$

Since c_1 is not a coalition candidate, this implies that $c_m = c_{3,2} = \ldots = c_{m,m-1}$—that is, the elements on the interior diagonal immediately left of the main diagonal are all identical to c_m, the candidate that heads the second row—by the reasoning of theorem 1. And c_m is also not a coalition candidate, so likewise c_{m-1} $= c_{4,2} = \ldots = c_{m,m-2}$—that is, the elements on the interior diagonal immediately left of the last one are all identical to c_{m-1}, the candidate that heads row 3.

Applying the same reasoning successively to $c_{m-1}, \ldots, c_4$, $(C_{i,j})$ must be of the form

$$(C_{i,j}) = \begin{bmatrix} c_1 & c_{1,2} & c_{1,3} & \cdots & & c_{1,m-1} & c_{1,m} \\ c_m & c_1 & c_{2,3} & \cdots & & c_{2,m-1} & c_{2,m} \\ c_{m-1} & c_m & c_1 & \cdots & & c_{3,m-1} & c_{3,m} \\ \vdots & & & & & & \\ c_4 & \cdots & \cdots & \cdots & \cdots & \cdots & \cdots \\ c_3 & c_4 & \cdots & c_{m-1} & c_m & c_1 & \cdots \\ c_2 & c_3 & c_4 & c_{m-2} & c_{m-1} & c_m & c_1 \end{bmatrix}$$

Since we can interchange rows *ad libitum*, we can put the first row of $(C_{i,j})$ into the last row, and the new matrix will be

$$\begin{bmatrix} c_m & c_1 & c_{2,3} & \cdots & & c_{2,m-1} & c_{2,m} \\ c_{m-1} & c_m & c_1 & \cdots & & c_{3,m-1} & c_{3,m} \\ \vdots & & & & & & \\ c_2 & c_3 & \cdots & \cdots & & c_m & c_1 \\ c_1 & c_{1,2} & \cdots & \cdots & & c_{1,m-1} & c_{1,m} \end{bmatrix}$$

Since it is a matrix of the system, $c_m = c_{1,m}$, $c_{m-1} = c_{1,m-1}, \ldots, c_3$ $= c_{1,3}$, and $c_2 = c_{1,2}$. Continuing this process, $(C_{i,j})$ must be of the form

$$\begin{bmatrix} c_1 & c_2 & \cdots & \cdots & \cdots & \cdots & c_{m-1} & c_m \\ c_m & c_1 & c_2 & \cdots & \cdots & \cdots & c_{m-2} & c_{m-1} \\ c_{m-1} & c_m & c_1 & c_2 & \cdots & \cdots & c_{m-3} & c_{m-2} \\ \vdots & & \vdots & & & \vdots & & \vdots \\ c_4 & \cdots & \cdots & \cdots & \cdots & c_1 & c_2 & c_3 \\ c_3 & c_4 & \cdots & \cdots & \cdots & c_m & c_1 & c_2 \\ c_2 & c_3 & c_4 & \cdots & \cdots & c_{m-1} & c_m & c_1 \end{bmatrix}$$

We call this a *circular* matrix. Notice the northwest to southeast diagonals, and that each row is obtained from the preceding row by a circular permutation.

Theorem 2. (Main Theorem) A normal, standard system is anarchic if and only if it has a circular matrix.

Proof. The preceding discussion establishes that a system has a circular matrix if it is normal, standard, and anarchic. It is further clear that if a system has a circular matrix, it is normal, standard, and anarchic. $[N(c_1, c_2) = m - 1, \ldots, N(c_i, c_{i+1}) = m - 1, \ldots, N(c_m, c_1) = m - 1.]$ Q.E.D.

Corollary. The paradox of voting has a circular matrix.

Comment: Since the paradox of voting is normal, standard, and anarchic it has a 3×3 circular matrix. Thus, $N(c_1, c_2) = m - 1 = 2, N(c_2, c_3) = m - 1 = 2$, and $N(c_3, c_1) = m - 1 = 2$, and majority preference is cyclical. Given a sense of "explanation" in which to show how a resultant, complex feature of a system follows from some of its more elementary features is to explain why the system has the complex feature; this explains why majority preference is cyclical in the paradox of voting.

II. Generalizing the Account

Since the previous reasoning involves special systems—normal, standard, and anarchic—it might be thought that our explanation lacks sufficient generality to be of much interest. The paradox of voting, fascinating as it is, is not the only majority preference cycle. They come in various shapes and sizes, not all with such nice, tame, symmetrical matrices.

Appendix

In fact, our approach can be extended, not by eliminating appeal to these special, symmetrical matrices, but by showing them to be "embedded" in a wide variety of settings. For instance, in every majority preference cycle with an odd number of voters there has to be an embedded paradox of voting. Majority preference, in such a setting, could not cycle otherwise. So our explanation of the paradox of voting covers more than just the paradox of voting.

We now extend our account to explain majority preference cycles in any setting with an odd number of voters. Recall that a candidate c_i is a majority candidate if $N(c_i, c_j) > [m/2]$ for all $c_j \neq c_i$, where m is the number of voters. Thus, if a system does not have a majority candidate, then for each candidate c_i there is a candidate c_j such that $N(c_j, c_i) \geq [m/2]$. We denote $N(c_i, c_j) \geq [m/2]$ by $c_j \leftarrow c_i$ or $c_i \rightarrow c_j$. A subset $\{c_1, \ldots, c_k\}$ of C is called a *loop of k elements* or a *k-loop* if $c_1 \rightarrow c_2 \rightarrow \ldots \rightarrow c_k \rightarrow c_1$.

Theorem 3. If a system does not have a majority candidate then either it has a 2-loop—i.e., it contains some c_i, c_j such that $N(c_i, c_j) = N(c_j, c_i) = [m/2]$—or it has a 3-loop: $c_1 \rightarrow c_2 \rightarrow c_3 \rightarrow c_1$ with the property that $N(c_1, c_2) > [m/2]$, $N(c_2, c_3) > [m/2]$, and $N(c_3, c_1) > [m/2]$.

Proof. Suppose the system contains no c_i, c_j for which $N(c_i, c_j) = N(c_j, c_i)$. Then for any distinct c_i and c_j, if $N(c_i, c_j) \not> [m/2]$ then $N(c_j, c_i) > [m/2]$. Since there is no majority candidate, for any c_1 in C we can choose a c_2 where $c_1 \leftarrow c_2$, and a c_3 where $c_1 \leftarrow c_2 \leftarrow c_3$, and so on. By this process we obtain $c_1 \leftarrow c_2 \leftarrow c_3 \leftarrow c_4 \leftarrow \ldots$. Since C is a finite set, there exists a k such that $c_1 \leftarrow c_2 \leftarrow c_3 \leftarrow \ldots \leftarrow c_k \leftarrow c_d$, where $1 \leq d \leq k$. If we relabel the c's, we obtain a loop: $c_1 \rightarrow c_2 \rightarrow c_3 \rightarrow \ldots \rightarrow c_L \rightarrow c_1$. If $N(c_1, c_3) > [m/2]$, then we can delete c_2 and obtain a $(L - 1)-$loop: $c_1 \rightarrow c_3 \rightarrow \cdots$

→ c_L → c_1. If, on the other hand, $N(c_1, c_3) \not> [m/2]$, then $N(c_3, c_1)$ > $[m/2]$ and we obtain a 3-loop: c_1 → c_2 → c_3 → c_1. Thus, the system always has a 3-loop—either by exhaustive deletions, or by discovering one sooner—with the property that $N(c_1, c_2)$ > $[m/2]$, $N(c_2, c_3)$ > $[m/2]$, and $N(c_3, c_1)$ > $[m/2]$. Q.E.D.

Theorem 4. If c_1 → c_2 → c_3 → c_1 is a 3-loop with the property that $N(c_1, c_2)$ > $[m/2]$, $N(c_2, c_3)$ > $[m/2]$, and $N(c_3, c_1)$ > $[m/2]$, then there exists some voter v_i in V where the chain of v_i in $\{c_1, c_2, c_3\}$ is $c_1 > c_2 > c_3$.

Proof. Let $(C_{i,j})$ be a matrix of the subsystem V and $\{c_1, c_2, c_3\}$. $(C_{i,j})$ is an $m \times$ matrix. c_1 must appear at least once in the first column of $(C_{i,j})$; otherwise, either c_2 or c_3 would appear $\geq [m/2]$ times in the first column, which contradicts either $N(c_1, c_2)$ > $[m/2]$ or $N(c_2, c_3)$ > $[m/2]$. So let $\{v_1, \ldots, v_h\}$ be the subset of V in which each chain of v_i has c_1 in the first position. The subsystem V and $\{c_1, c_2, c_3\}$ thus has a matrix of the form

$$
\begin{array}{c}
v_1: \\
\vdots \\
v_h: \\
\\
\\
\end{array}
\begin{bmatrix}
c_1 & c_{1,2} & c_{1,3} \\
\vdots & \vdots & \vdots \\
c_1 & c_{h,2} & c_{h,3} \\
\vdots & \vdots & \vdots \\
c_{m,1} & c_{m,2} & c_{m,3}
\end{bmatrix}
$$

Since there is no majority candidate, no candidate can appear more than $[m/2]$ times in the first column, and each must appear at least once. Hence, the number of first position appearances of any two candidates added together will be $\geq [m/2]$. So c_3 cannot appear in second position in all the rows c_1 appears first in, because adding together all its first and second position appearances we would have $N(c_2, c_3) \not> [m/2]$, contrary to the hypothesis. Thus, at least one $c_{i,2} = c_2$, $1 \leq i \leq h$. The chain of v_i is then $c_1 > c_2 > c_3$. Q.E.D.

We will call a subsystem $\{V', C'\}$ *circular* if it has a circular matrix. If $c_1 \rightarrow c_2 \rightarrow c_3 \rightarrow c_1$ is a 3-loop with the property that $N(c_1, c_2) > [m/2]$, $N(c_2, c_3) > [m/2]$, and $N(c_3, c_1) > [m/2]$, then $c_3 \rightarrow c_1 \rightarrow c_2 \rightarrow c_3$ and $c_2 \rightarrow c_3 \rightarrow c_1 \rightarrow c_2$ are also such loops. By theorem 4 there exists $\{v_1, v_2, v_3\}$ such that the subsystem $\{v_1, v_2, v_3\}$ and $\{c_1, c_2, c_3\}$ is circular.

Theorem 5. If a system does not have a majority candidate, then either there is some c_i, c_j such that $N(c_i, c_j) = N(c_j, c_i) = [m/2]$ (which can happen only when the number of voters is even), or the system has a circular subsystem consisting of three voters and three candidates (that is, an embedded paradox of voting).

Theorem 6. If a system with an odd number of voters lacks a majority candidate, then every candidate in the system is a member of an embedded paradox of voting.

Proof. In the second sentence of the proof of theorem 3, there are no restrictions on which candidate we start with. So the theorem holds for any candidate. Therefore, this result follows by theorems 3, 4, and 5.

Index

Absolute, principle of the, $114n$–$15n$
Aggregation device, 1–11, 13–14, 25, 38, 62, 103; dictatorial, 22, 105, 107, 108, 111; and global information, 94, 97–98, 99–100, 101; and infinite regress, 114, 117, 118–19, 120–22, 125; and noncreativity, 78–80, 83–88; vicious, 105–11, 114, 117, 119, 122, 125. See also Comparisons; Polyathlon scoring; Voting
Anarchic setting, 129, 130–35
Appropriate responsiveness, 23–24
Aquinas, Thomas, $113n$
Arbitrariness, 64–65, 73, 84–85, 86–87
Aristotle, 4, $114n$, 125
Asymmetry, 115, 117, 118, 119, 123–24
Athletic scoring, 14–42 passim, 48, 61–71, 76–77, 78–79
Austin, J. L., $5n$
Automanipulability, 45–46

Beliefs, intuitive, 113
Beth, E. W., $114n$–$15n$
Black, Duncan, $27n$, 28, $90n$
Brandt, R. B., $75n$, $76n$
Butler, Joseph, 45

Candidates, 105; coalition, 129, 130, 132–33, 134; dead, 78–79, 80–82; majority, 128, 130, 136, 137, 138
Cardinality, 9–10, $20n$, 77, 88; in athletic scoring, 16, 17, 41, 65, 66, 70–71; and interpersonal comparisons, 65, 66, 70–72, 73, 74–75, 76; in rank-order voting, 35, 83, 84
Churchman, C. W., $76n$
Circular matrix, 106, 128, 134–38
Citizens' sovereignty (CS), 104–05
Coalition candidate, 129, 130, 132–33, 134
Coalition: majority, 93–94, 129; simple, 129
Coffee-sweetness analogy, 50–51, 52–55, 57, 59
Collective choice, 1, 8–9, 13, 25, 103; and dictatorial devices, 22; and preference intensity, 9, 43, 72
Collective rationality, 5, $7n$. See also Rationality
Comparisons: interevent, 39, 40–41, 61–70, 76–77; intergroup, 73–76; interpersonal, 47–48, 61–77, 91
Conceptual description, 60
Conditional contraries, 121
Condorcet, Marquis de, 26–27
Connectedness, $7n$, $18n$, 104, 107, 121

139

Index

Index